Heaven and Angels

Schoenbeck is author of:

The Final Entrance: Journeys beyond Life

Near-Death Experiences: Visits to the Other Side

Good Grief: Daily Meditations: A Book of Caring and Remembrance

Zen and the Art of Nursing

Learn more about Susan Schoenbeck at susanschoenbeck.com. Watch Susan's website for links to Instagram and blog.

Heaven

and

Angels

Susan L. Schoenbeck RN, MSN

Published by Springwater Press

Silverton Oregon

Springwaterpress.com

Dedicated to those whose stories are woven in this book into a tapestry of hope.

Table of Contents

Introduction

This book is written for everyday people who want to learn more about love, forgiveness, and hope.

Healthcare professionals such as nurses, social workers, chaplains, nursing assistants, medics, police personnel, firefighters and doctors who want to expand their awareness of the values, beliefs and experiences of folks for whom they care will find the stories within this book a guide for better understanding the perspectives of those they serve.

Few things are more feared than death. Experiences with death haunt some people. Thoughts of death torture others. Nothing is more painful than the sense of loss we feel when someone we love dies. Death is a big part of life.

Although death has been around just about as long as life has, we talk more openly about the joy of birthing than about the sacred process of dying. But, the rise of "death cafes" and interest in "natural burial rites" tell us that people do want a picture of what dying is like. And, individuals aspire to prepare themselves. So, to meet this demand for knowledge, *Heaven and Angels* presents the penultimate of all life experiences — the far edge of death — heaven.

Many of the stories revealed in this book were derived from my clinical work as a bedside intensive care (ICU) nurse, clinical nurse specialist for death and spiritual care, teacher, Director of Nursing, and state nursing home investigator. People who survived accidents and cardiopulmonary resuscitation (CPR) and had near-death experiences (NDEs) shared with me their visions of the other side. Accounts also come from those who have witnessed the life-death juncture up close.

Some people do not believe in heaven. Some people think nothing exists after death. Death is the final chapter; the book is finished. Others believe that death, when one is elderly, is part of a natural ending to life, and that, at least some parts of healthcare today, interfere in that process. Many believe that even though people die, they may return to visit in a spiritual form.

Those individuals who can obtain all their material needs and wants are now turning their attention to spiritual questions about existence. They ask what lies ahead at the end of this earthly journey. This book has the answers for them.

All major religions talk about an afterlife. So do those who have been close to death. People who have been clinically dead and resuscitated often declare, "I know. I met God. I talked to Jesus." And, dying people often exclaim to spirits who reach out and talk to them from an existence hidden to us, "I am coming soon to join you. I see the angels waiting for me."

As a child stricken with polio, I left my body when I was in pain and floated above it in a spirit form. I watched and heard what was going on around my body. I learned early on that there is another realm of existence. Supernatural encounters taught me at a very young age that angels and Jesus do come to those in need.

When I became a nurse and spent time at the side of people during death, I often heard references to a light that guided people on their way to heaven. The dying talked about seeing a light. Many who survived CPR, described a light-being that bathed them in unconditional love.

I studied the Bible to examine references to a light. Scriptures support there is a light that serves as a beacon guiding the dying to heaven. People who have met this holy light report they feel a love and peace that exceeds all their previous understanding. They say death is a journey to a place where physical pain, anxiety, shame and psychological hurt no longer exist.

Comforting passages from the Bible are incorporated into this text. Readers may want to share these scriptures with dying loved ones.

A common thread in people's stories about heaven and angels is the presence of very special people on earth. Everyday people can be a light on earth for others. And that is the point, after all…that we follow in the footsteps of Jesus to be an inspiring, forgiving person of unconditional love and acceptance.

As you read the stories of people who have seen angels and heaven, I invite you to awaken yourself to the love, forgiveness and hope that these accounts bring. Michelangelo cautioned us to not dread death as it comes from the same maker as life. We need not fear death for, by all these accounts, it leads to heaven.

Susan L. Schoenbeck, RN MSN

My Story

He leadeth me beside the still waters. He restoreth my soul.

Psalm 23

I know about the track to heaven because I am a nurse who has been at the precipice of death, caring for the dying and those who have come back from clinical death after emergency care such as resuscitation. I have also spent many hours consoling the grieving…meeting families in the hospital as they are told their loved ones are dead.

My special insight comes from the fact that I listened and recognized the Christian commonalities their stories shared. At the bedsides of the dying, I witnessed patients talking to loved ones who had died before them. I couldn't see the people to whom they spoke. I listened to dying patients describe the heaven they saw when they readied to cross over from life into death. I heard patients who had been resuscitated tell of being in conversation with God in heaven during the time they were declared clinically dead. It has been a gift to sit beside people who speak of their loved ones, God and Jesus who live in heaven. The stories in this book share their voices with you.

Why did I believe these patients' reports of heaven? In part, I encountered elements of heaven and Jesus at a very early age. I contracted polio when I was six months old. I have always had a lot of pain from the base of my spine through my legs. As a child, when experiencing excruciating pain, my body lay fixed on its back, motionless because one leg was caged in a metal brace so heavy I could not roll over. At these times, I moved out of my body to a place where I would float in spirit form above my body until the pain subsided. I would journey and meet angels. I met Jesus who was with the angels. This was a fine lesson for me. My learning underscores that people often learn and grow in strength and conviction through distressing experiences. And Jesus comforts those who suffer.

I was brought up in a Christian household where a booklet of daily scriptures was placed on the breakfast table for all to read. Each page contained a Bible verse followed by a paragraph relating how that scripture could influence our day. My father's directive for leading a good life was: think, plan, work, study, play and rest. The scriptures were meant guide us how to live this life well.

My nursing practice started in a cardiovascular surgical ICU. In other words, we took care of patients who had heart surgery. Many times, their hearts, irritated by all the poking and prodding surgery entails, stopped. We did CPR and brought the patients "back to life." One particular time, a patient told me she had been out of her body watching me do CPR. She said that, during the CPR, she was pain-free and floating above and looking down at the scene. She reported that she could hear everything said as doctors and nurses joined in the resuscitation effort. She talked of going to "all the way to heaven and back."

Other nurses poked fun at me for believing the patient. Some said that the patient was probably having a dream made up by her mind to make her feel okay during this life-threatening event. Several thought that at the time of CPR, the patient was not getting enough blood to her brain causing a phantom belief that she separated from her body. Still others said, "Sue, you have no proof."

Because of my own childhood experiences, I was open to hearing the voices of patients who had crossed over and came back when they told me they talked with angels and Jesus. I believe patients sensed they could talk to me because, just like a parent who loses a child will seamlessly bond with others who have lost a child, I was open to hearing because I also experienced the same.

Frankly, the physiological and/or psychological rationale underlying a person's seeing heaven and angels and talking to God and Jesus does not matter. These experiences are real to the persons experiencing them. As a nurse, it is the person's world I must enter in order to help them. The patient's perspective is their reality.

What do patients tell nurses? They talk of going out of their bodies, looking down at the scene below, and traveling down a tunnel into a bright light. Many say the light is a being – God or Jesus – who is loving and welcoming. As a nurse, it was natural for me to listen to patients' stories. I also interviewed patients who had been in accidents and/or whose hearts had stopped and were resuscitated. I talked with patients who had NDEs. This research was published in the *Journal of Near-Death Studies.* At the time of this research, I did not fully realize that the visions of light near-death experiencers (NDERs) had were encounters with heaven. Stories I have collected about NDEs can be found in my book, *Near-Death Experiences: Visits to the Other Side.*

I am an oblate—which is a community member—of the Benedictine Holy Wisdom Monastery. Nuns are in charge of the monastery. They invite members of the community to join them in worship, work, study and monastery activities. Each day at the monastery starts and ends with lectio—a reading of scripture along with meditation on the words of the passage, singing of hymns and personal reflection. As part of my study at the monastery, I read a book that listed all references to tight in the Bible. I found the verses about heavenly light comforting and have included some scriptures throughout this manuscript in hope that the reader may find these passages soothing and reassuring. I anticipate the reader will also find the scriptures captivating and comforting. Let the scriptures ripple through you—inspiring and defining your thoughts and feelings.

The packaging of death has changed dramatically in recent decades giving us more people to talk to about their experiences during clinical death. Advances in technology have allowed people to arrive at the edge of death, experience some of heaven, and to be pulled back through medical intervention. Because people now receive vital treatment so quickly, their mental faculties often are not impaired. They return to life and can tell stories about their heavenly journey that in the past have been lost either to death, to permanent brain damage or, perhaps also to fear of telling the tale.

The stories of the dying and those who have returned from clinical death events give vivid reports of a heavenly realm that co-exists with our earthly world. Their stories share common themes. When the perilous event, such as a heart attack, car accident or war injury occurred, survivors exited their earthly bodies and floated above the scene. They had no pain. They were surprised to look down and see and hear people gathered around their earthly bodies. The near-death experiencers told of travel through a tunnel at the end of which was a bright light. Many spoke of this light-being as "God" or "Jesus." This deity enveloped them in unconditional love.

NDE travelers also spoke of meeting family and friends and watching a playback of key events in their lives. The near-death experiencers said that there was no language yet everyone's thoughts were understood. No language was needed. They reported there is a review of deeds in the form of questions such as:

- What good have you done with your life?

- How did you use your talents?

- Who did you love the most?

- What events made you grow the most?

- When did you turn around and forgive a person who wronged you?

I call this the "golden rule" review of deeds because the questions focus on how a person treated others. What we do for others counts. What happens in life—the good and bad--helps us grow in wisdom. God and Jesus accept people as they are—something we humans have a hard time doing. Jesus helped those who others rejected…those sick with contagious disease, the lame, and the harlots whose behaviors arose not so much from within but from the circumstances and social pressures they faced.

The Language of Grief

I began to use the facts learned from my own life experiences, the glimpses of heaven dying patients reported, and the experiences of people who went onto heaven and returned, to console loved ones left behind. When families come to the emergency room (ER) and find out someone they loved has died, they have questions.

The most frequently asked question is, "Did my loved one have pain at the end?" We, who know and understand how trips to heaven and back work, can answer that query with certainty. Reports from motor vehicle accident victims, from people fleeing dangerous situations, from those on the battlefield concur that when a person dies, all pain ceases. So I began to use this fact to comfort those who grieve.

When I was a clinical nurse specialist for death and spiritual care for a hospital, I met ambulances with a chaplain. The families had just been told their loved ones were dead or were likely to die. These scenes were horrible. I struggled at first with what to say to console them. Those who lost loved ones often met me with vacant stares. They shuddered. They moaned. They pounded on the walls. Parents who lost children were the worst off. Their loss was like a bloody, gaping wound. No one could fix that.

One particular event got me started using the words of the dying and the near-death experiencers to help those who grieve. I was in the ER with parents who had just been told their child had died at the babysitter's house. The preliminary diagnosis was Sudden Infant Death Syndrome (SIDS). The parents were seated in a private area. The mother would not make eye contact with anyone. She bent her body, curling it forward into a ball as she cried. She rocked back and forth, back and forth in her chair. The father stared forward as if looking at something I could not see. I was kneeling on the floor next to a chaplain.

The rocking and the wailing continued. No one really talked in the beginning. I know I was thinking, "What can I possibly say to help people who have lost a child?"

When the crying let up I explained how people who clinically died and were resuscitated said that they popped out of their body into a spirit form in which they felt no pain. I hoped this message— answering the number one question family members have when a loved one has died– would comfort them. The family did not immediately respond so I could not tell. Our eyes still had not met. Weeping again filled the space between us until, after a few minutes, the father looked at me and said, "I am glad Jenny did not have pain when she died." All of us except the mother nodded. The mother still rocked back and forth my message seemingly ignored by her.

I took a chance and again filled the gap between us by talking more about what I had been told by those who had died and returned to life. I mentioned how near-death experiencers were met on the other side by welcoming family and loved ones. I told the family that those who went to heaven in clinical death and returned often reported meeting God and Jesus. Only then did the mother stop weeping and look up. She said to her husband, "She would be safe with Jesus. Do you think your mother was there for her?" The father took his wife in his arms and said, "Yes, that is probably what happened. I can see my mother meeting Jenny." The husband told us that his mother had died six months ago.

The lessons the dying and those who survived terrible accidents and CPR voiced helped this family learn their child was not alone when she died. The child would have been met by God, Jesus and/or her grandmother. The family was consoled knowing their daughter did not suffer pain when she died. Glimpses of heaven and talks with God and Jesus shared with me by those who experienced it were now helping a family cope with a world previously unknown to them. Perhaps that is one of the reasons dying people talk aloud as they cross over into death and near-death experiencers tell their stories—so others touched by death may be comforted.

While I was a Director of Nursing, a Christian staff member experienced the death of his child. In a sympathy card, I enclosed three index cards containing facts related to death learned over the course of my nursing career. Some of these truths came from listening to the dying and those who had been in accidents and/or resuscitated. Other facts came from my readings and research on near-death events.

Several days after receiving the three cards, the man came back and asked me if he could have three more of these cards. "Your notes helped me," he said. I said I could have the cards written for him by the end of the day. I gave the man a few more passages. Days later he again he returned seeking more cards and said, "My wife and I share your words. We'd love to read any others you might have." So I wrote more cards for him and his wife. He came back, saying, "Your statements mimic exactly what we are feeling. How do you know what we are feeling?" I replied that I learned about heaven by listening to those who had seen it or been there. And, what I heard matched scriptures. God, Jesus and loved ones who died before would be there in heaven for his son.

For one year, my writing for this man and woman continued. The family kept all the cards and notes in a binder. I wrote special messages for holidays and for the birthday of their son. The son was a guitarist. The father gave me a CD of his son's music. I played it for inspiration. I did not realize it at the time but I was becoming the scribe connecting this family who lost their son to the voices of the dying, accident survivors and the near-death experiencers. And I was sharing my voice, too, for I know that heaven is real. I composed words for daily meditation to help the man and his wife to talk to their son. I had no intention to write a book. But, indeed, this is how *Good Grief: Daily Meditations: A Book of Caring and Remembrance* began…one day at a time.

In turn, this family taught me that creating a time and space for such remembrance was healing. So I continued sharing factual information in each meditation, but also added an affirmation— words of lament, of forgiveness, of wonderment…words this man and his wife could use to express what they were experiencing. Their grief was now linked to words that showed recognition of their feelings…words they could not find on their own.

The man also used the meditations to talk with his son at graveside. People walking by glanced surreptitiously at him. At first, the man felt uncomfortable. But, then, I counseled him saying, "Let's face it. We all talk to loved ones who died. It's normal. Heaven knows they can hear us." So he continued, ignoring the glances of passersby. Talking to his son made him feel connected with him. And this was a good emotion. He knew his son was still there... just somewhere beyond sight...not beyond reach.

Whereas other folks were telling this family to accept the loss of their son and move on, I was saying, "Let go of letting go of your loved one. Remember him. Think about you and him...your relationship...how his death is forcing you to reflect on your life. Talk to him and you will know in your mind what he would say." When loved ones are no longer with us physically, they continue to influence us. We feel their presence.

I do not doubt people communicate with spirits beyond life. I see the relief on mourners' faces when told they do not need to accept their loss, bury it and just move on. They're gratified others understand and accept that talking about and talking with a loved one who has died is healthy. Such remembrance is healing.

The couple later wrote to me, "Though your writings often make us cry, they say things that are hard for us to express. The pain of losing our son is almost unbearable at times, but it is comforting to know there is someone that truly understands. You have taken us a step beyond grief." I myself began to understand that I was learning my whole life how to help people understand that heaven exists and that God and Jesus were in heaven. I realized that I could share with those who have lost loved ones a place beyond grief that I fortuitously experienced throughout my life.

So *Good Grief: Daily Meditations: A Book of Caring and Remembrance* with its language of grief emerged from my own childhood experiences and the collective voices of near-death experiencers, the dying on their deathbeds and those who shared their grief with me. The words came from their hearts: Simple words. Tender truths revealing what was in their minds and souls. Just ordinary words strung together in the language of grief.

This book, *Heaven and Angels*, contains stories of people I have talked to in my role as a staff nurse, clinical nurse specialist for death and spiritual care, Director of Nursing, state nursing home investigator, and as nursing faculty in colleges of nursing. It is written so you may know what many people earnestly say exists beyond this life in heaven:

Angels, God, and Jesus along with our loved ones who have gone before us.

It is often a mystery to us how we have come to know and believe in certain things. Beliefs are like guests who come up to your door. They come in only if you open the door and invite them in. Maybe that is why you are reading this book…to gain an understanding of life after death.

My life experiences, though not chosen by me, taught me how to help people understand that at death we exit our earthbound forms and go to heaven. My pathway in life has been to experience, to listen, to pay attention to commonalities in people's stories, to remember, to record and re-tell. I do this with the appreciation that heaven and angels exist.

> *For it is by grace you have been saved,*
> *through faith—and this not from yourselves,*
> *it is the gift of God—not by works, so that no*
> *one can boast. For we are God's*
> *workmanship, created in Christ Jesus to do*
> *good works, which God prepared in advance*
> *for us to do.*
>
> *Ephesians 2: 8-10*

The Angels Pay a Visit

And I beheld, and I heard the voice of many angels round about the throne and the beasts and the elders; and the number of them was ten thousand times ten thousand, and thousands and thousands.

Revelations 5:11

I was a nursing home investigator called out on a case where the evening before a patient had died accidentally by getting her nightgown caught in the side rail. At times like these, when unintended deaths occur, "somber" is not a powerful enough word to describe the circulating emotions. Each staff member is second guessing themselves, wondering if there was something they could have done to prevent the incident.

The deceased must have been trying to get out of bed, when a tie on her gown got caught within a mechanism that controlled the bars on the side rail. She literally hung her body when the tie caught within the lever. Her body was not tall enough to reach the floor to allow her to stand and thus, avoid suffocation.

But this was not the whole story and I will tell you why. At the end of the day, my partner and I were gathering up our papers when a nursing assistant asked if she could speak to us. She was just coming onto her shift and had heard about the unfortunate death. Since death and dying was my specialty, the other inspector said, "Sure, tell Sue your story."

I sat down with the nursing assistant who described what she was doing the evening the death occurred:

> "I work the 4 pm to 8 pm shift. I was just coming back from an activity with the patient whose room is directly across the room from the woman who died. One of my duties

is to get my patients ready for bed before I
leave my shift.

The patient I was bringing back to her
room has a pleasant dementia. She is always
smiling and cooperative. When I wheeled her
back to her room at a little before eight, she
was in a chipper mood. I was surprised when
she suddenly balked at letting me turn the
wheelchair into her room. She said that she
wanted to stay in the hallway and watch the
angels. I questioned, 'The angels?' The patient
pointed to the ceiling above the doorway of
the room of the patient who hung and died.
The patient with dementia told me clearly that
she wanted to stay up to watch the angels. She
said, 'See the angels…over there by the light.'
I tried to reason with her. Although I did not
want to disregard her perception, I did not
believe she was really looking at angels. I
looked toward the place where she stared. I
did not see any light other than the regular
hallway lighting. I encouraged her to comply
with my request. I cajoled her. I told her I
would get in trouble if I did not get her in bed.
But, she would not budge.

I couldn't make the patient go into her room so I left my shift at 8 pm with the patient sitting forward in her chair her chin resting on her elbows propped up on her knees. She sat in the hallway smiling broadly and gazing at the ceiling near the doorway across the hall. I said 'Good night. See you tomorrow.' The patient disregarded me. Instead, she waved her hand and called out, 'Oh, joy. Oh, joy.' When I got to work today, I heard about what happened last night and I felt a need to tell someone. So here I am. The other inspector seemed to think you would understand. Do you?"

The nursing assistant asked me if a patient with dementia could have actually seen something that was not apparent to her. I assured the nursing assistant that there are times when patients tell us they can see into a world beyond ours. Nurses describe patients with dementia perceiving things ordinary people may not. It is as if the patient with dementia is in another space in time. Nurses recount hearing the dying talking to people they describe as angels in heaven.

So is the story believable? I think so. Evidence is on the side of angels being with people as they cross over into heaven. Research reveals people report seeing, hearing and feeling the movement from the wings of angels around the time of death. This story reinforces that no one really dies alone. Angels may help us with the crossover into heaven. Angels also comfort those left behind like the patient with dementia. People come into our lives for a reason. Sometimes, it is to bring us knowledge or insight we could not find on our own. The nursing assistant let out a sigh of relief, "I wanted to believe," she said. "Now I can."

> *Then the seventh angel blew his trumpet, and there were loud voices in heaven, saying, The kingdom of the world has become the kingdom of our Lord and of his Christ, and he shall reign forever and ever.*
>
> *Revelations 11:15*

Destination Heaven

Send out your light and your truth to be my guide. Let them lead me to your holy hill, to your dwelling place.

Psalm 43:3

The family came to me saying their father was tired and wanted to die. He was sick enough to die, according to the doctors. He had hospice care. But it had been months since he was expected to die and had not. The family sought advice because the 92-year-old father was having "trouble dying".

I met several times with the man before he left his earthly body. It's important to take stock of your life from time to time. He was having some anxious moments doing so. The man talked of wanting to join his wife in heaven. His view of heaven came from his religion. He believed good people went to heaven when they died and bad people went to hell.

He knew his wife was in heaven because he believed no one led such a good life as she had. She raised happy children. She held a responsible position at respected company. She was a hard worker. She was nice to everyone. Any complaints she had were justified. She never yelled. She had died ten years ago. Hers was an unexpected death for him. He thought he would go first.

In his younger days he was the family member who made sure the children got to church and catechism lessons. He ushered in church on Sundays as a measure of his willingness to be a servant of God. Being part of the church defined the man. For him, God was the Father and Jesus, his Son, was the role model for how people should behave toward one another. Following the teachings of Jesus, he did volunteer work with the less fortunate in the community.

Now, however, some knotty life situations he had been involved in worried him. He had spent large sums of money indiscriminately. He openly talked about being tormented that what he had done would not be forgiven. I reminded him God is a loving and forgiving being. He said he knew this. He was worried his wife was the one who would feel betrayed and unhappy with his actions.

Sometimes it is hard to let go of the past. Shame, and our secrecy about it, cause fear. But what is in the past cannot be undone. You cannot re-enter it. Going forward is the only way to go. I tried to help him with this concern by saying that we all are scared that others will know we have made mistakes. We are not always the person we want others to believe us to be. It is hard sometimes for our minds to let go of our past blunders. But, to go on— we must do just that. And, each of us can take heart that we are not alone. God the Father and Jesus will never leave our side. And, those we love in life who also want to follow the teachings of Jesus, will always love us despite our faults. Knowing how we wish our own failures to be forgiven, may make us more understanding of the weaknesses of others.

Rather than living in a world of regret, I encouraged him to picture the reality of heaven before him and to step into that comforting space. My experiences holding the hands of the dying have taught me that oftentimes those we have loved who have died before us come to be by our side when it is our turn to cross over. Again and again, the dying report they have visions of loved ones being near. Dying people declared their dead loved ones talk to them. Loved ones tell the dying they soon will be able to join them in heaven. So, I asked the man if he had seen his wife lately.

The man turned his head in annoyance and averted his eyes. He mumbled as he turned away. In an effort to give the man permission to talk about such an experience, I told the man that we, nurses, talk to people who tell us their spouses who have died come and talk to them. People left behind after the deaths of spouses sometimes smell the scents of their loved ones and feel that they are present.

Almost fifty percent of interviewed spouses reported after-death-communication. I then backed off. At least I had planted the seed that a meeting with his wife could happen. Having heard only of pleasant interactions between deceased and living spouses, I hoped in my heart such a meeting would comfort him.

When I returned, a day or so later, I found the man with his head down and his shoulders slumped over the night stand. The man said to me, "I am still having trouble dying." I said I was sorry about this and would pray he could die in his sleep as he voiced he wanted. I inquired if he had seen his wife lately. The man straightened up and looked me in the eye and said, "She came to me. I saw her. I haven't told anyone. I didn't want to tell you last time you were here. People will think I am a crazy old man. I don't want my kids to be told their father is dumb or mixed up."

I tried to reframe his experience saying, "But, that's wonderful, you saw her." I probed for further information asking if he talked to his wife about the worrisome feelings he had. He said, "No, I did not." But, he continued, "She talks to me kindly and tells me everything will be okay."

I encouraged the man to believe her, and said, "No matter how we fall down here on earth, God understands and sends angels to help us get back up again. That's how it works. We all fall down. With the grace of God's help, we get back up again. From what you describe, your wife always has been an angel. She will not be angry with you." After a few minutes of silence, the old man said, "Yes. I guess I was forgetting that she was an angel on earth. And, obviously, now, if what you say is true, I am seeing her as a real heavenly angel." I prayed the man would be strengthened by understanding her forgiveness.

I told him one of the many graces of God that happened at death was people we loved come to welcome us to heaven. I told him not to be afraid. He could expect his wife to come and meet him as he died. The man gently clasped my hand. He no longer carried the heavy weight of the anger he had presumed she had toward him.

We prayed the words of Luke 2:29-32:

Now, Lord, you are releasing your servant in peace, according to your promise. For I have seen with my own eyes the deliverance you have made ready in full view of all nations. A light that will bring revelation to the Gentiles and glory to your people Israel.

Luke 2:29-32

I touched base with the old man every few days. He voiced that he was "still trying hard to die." He grumbled he was in pain. He complained that his independence had long ago been taken away. But he clung to the joy that his wife was stopping in to see him. He refused to tell anyone but me of her visits.

It was obvious that facility staff could very well meet the man's bodily needs. But, what he most sought when he was dying, was reassurance he would be going to heaven and that visits from his wife meant God sent his wife, an angel, to meet him. The last time I talked with him he said he was close to going on. He could see his wife beckoning him. She said to him, "Come, now." His voice held a spark of eagerness when he said he saw a bright light around his wife. I told him he could let himself go into the light toward his wife. We prayed to Jesus for forgiveness for his wrongdoings.

The man became physically weaker and more anxious to die. He wanted relief from bodily pain. He yelled at others because he was angry he hurt so much. He swore. He did not see the sense for all the pain he suffered at the end. I assured him that his pain would be gone when he died. I explained that people who have gone out of their bodies during cardiopulmonary resuscitation, at accident scenes, when injured greatly in war, reported that they had no pain once their spirit left their body. I promised him pain would cease. He said he still was mad pain had to be at all. I had no real answer for this. The nurses treated his physical pain as best they could. But, it was the sorrow of pain the man seemed to question.

Why pain at all? Why so much pain for him at the end?

We discussed how Jesus role modeled helping others. I was able to weave in the stories the man and his family told me about how he went out of his way to help those in need so, in the end, the man would remember how he lessened others' pain. He lived the parable from Genesis about being "my brother's keeper".

Sometimes our worry about what is to come in the future hides the many meaningful things we have done in our lives from our view. All it takes is another person to talk about those acts of kindness and we are soothed. We can all do this for one another. We can recount for each other stories of the past that attach a sense of meaning to our lives.

The man spoke of his wife and the light every time I came to see him. I guess he figured I was comforted by knowing he was seeing them. I told him it was an okay time to go toward his wife and the light. And one night in his sleep, he did.

The Bible reinforces for us what the dying and those who have died and come back say in Isaiah 60:20:

Never again will your sun set nor the moon withdraw her light; but the Lord God will be your everlasting light and your days of mourning will be ended.

Isaiah 60:20

God's Word is a Lamp.

Your word is a lamp to my feet, a light on my path.

Psalm 119:105

Many patients knew without me telling them that their time of death was near. In fact, sometimes when things seemed calm—heart rates and rhythms were normal and blood pressures holding fine, I did not realize the patient was close to death. It is not unusual for healthcare staff to remark that when everything seems to be going favorably and the patient is calm and, even lucid, death can sweep in unexpectedly, quickly.

I worked in a Catholic hospital's coronary care unit (an intensive care unit for patients who had heart attacks and heart failure). I had many chances to observe the comfort this religion brought to people. There were always priests available to listen and console. With no special training in medicine, these men brought the light of the presence of God to the bedside. Many times, their words helped us nurses as much as the patients and families through emotion-laden times.

As priests read and explained scripture verses to people, I could see that patients became more relaxed. I saw God working through the priests to bring many dying patients and their family members' peace of mind. Sometimes, it is hard for the dying to put into words what they want to say as they move forward to heaven. I observed that it was often the priests who were able to bring forth the words that represented what was deep in the hearts of patients.

When priests brought the word of God to patients, I would often hear them quote Job 29:3:

When his lamp shone above my head and by its light, I walked through the darkness.

Job 29:3

The first view I had of this patient was that of a late-fiftyish appearing woman—arms folded tightly across her chest—being wheeled down a dimly lit hallway toward the coronary care unit. It was at the beginning of my shift. Her belongings... purse, clothing were on her lap. She gazed about as the transport person quickly moved her wheelchair with an intravenous line (IV) past one room and then another. I walked up to meet her. Her brow was furrowed as if in deep thought. She appeared weary, distracted and too tired to care that one shoulder of her gown had fallen down revealing her sharp clavicle freckled by age. Her cinnabar lips bespoke her desire to be pretty. Her eyes were a watery blue but she shed no tears. She was unaccompanied.

The transport person offered to assist her into bed but she said she wanted to do it herself. She was having trouble getting her left leg onto the mattress and used her arms to pull it up. "Old stroke," she said as if needing to give us a reason for her struggling. Her papers revealed she was in her early seventies, much older than she appeared. Her former occupation was listed as "ballerina, then mother." Loss of gracefulness with her illness had to have been a "little death" for her. Look at any older person and you can imagine the losses each has experienced as time weakens their strength and stability.

I asked if I could call anyone for her. "No," she said with a staccato response and a broad smile. Kids all live out-of-state. No need to worry them unnecessarily. Just have a stomachache that won't go away. I thought I would be going back to my apartment. Oh well, the doctors said I had no choice but to stay."

I had to quell any eagerness to inform the family as was the usual procedure. Her reasons for not informing her children were her own. It's a nurse's job to listen, understand, and help the patient reach their goals. Sometimes, the quieter you are, the better you hear what someone else wants.

The orders I received indicated the woman was to have a full cardiac work-up for possible heart-attack. For women, chest pain may not be the main sign of a heart attack. Instead, a stomachache may be the most notable sign of a heart attack that a woman experiences.

So, like others, this woman came with no expectation that her illness might be heart-related. That she was placed in a coronary care unit was a shock for her. But she was taking it stoically asking very intelligent questions about what each blood test could show. When a patient hears that the heart may be involved, the weightiness of their ailment increases their anxiety by leaps and bounds. Luckily, I could tell her that the EKG (electrocardiogram reading of her heart rate and rhythm) so far showed her heart rhythm was a normal pattern. She was given a "stable condition" ranking by the emergency room doctors.

Late evening fell, and the woman was not asleep. I made her a cup of herbal tea served with some graham crackers. I helped her put on hospital socks. People fall asleep more readily if their feet are warm. She laid her head back and closed her eyes folding her arms up by her chin under the extra blanket I gave her.

I was surprised when she stayed awake past ten o'clock. I offered to turn on a radio for her. Hospital music turns off at eight when visitors leave. It can become eerily quiet for some patients. I checked in on her to let her know her EKG was okay, her blood pressure was fine and it would be good for her to get some rest.

Around 2:30 in the morning, the woman put her call light on. She asked me if I would phone a priest to give her communion. At first, unaware of what was keeping the patient awake, I offered her a back rub and medicine to help her sleep. She declined both and asked me again to arrange for a priest to come. I was not sure what to do. The woman was in "stable condition". The priest's routine was to come at 0630 each morning. Sleep, I reasoned, would benefit her heart and, with respite, she would be in better shape to face a day ahead of more examinations and the results of tests run today.

But, she neither accepted my offerings nor looked away from me. Something crossed her face. She stared straight into my eyes as if I wasn't catching what she was saying. I was listening. Yet it took me moments to understand. Not sleep...she did not want sleep. She was asking for a priest. She did not want to trouble her children with her hospitalization. I considered this preference as independence. Later I thought that beneath her pleasant smile, she had been hiding her feeling she would die. Her stoicism was a mask. Her polite manners were deceiving. She wanted control.

This patient was like many of us who keep our emotions in check when we are very frightened. But, underneath our silence, when we are scared, a voice in each of us cries out for God to help us. On bad days when our world turns upside down, even if we have shorted God our time and our attention, we still, in a knee-jerk reaction, call out to Him. Isn't that what we expect of a Father? To be there always... even if we have may not have been. Maybe we do not ask that we or times be made better, but we ask for help to guide us to cope with whatever unpleasant thing is happening. We seek the touch and comfort of God. I have seen priests bring this to patients unceasingly...again and again through the reading of scripture.

Something in the woman's relentless gaze into my eyes corralled my thoughts. She spoke. I listened to what she was saying and also looked at her nonverbal communication. I recognized she had to have communion before any sleep was going to happen. I called the priest.

Calling a priest is easy. Getting him to come in the middle of the night...well, I was fortunate I worked at a place where priests unreservedly listened to nurses. I explained that the patient had not slept since she came into the coronary care unit just after dinner. I said, "She seems distracted. She doesn't want family called. She said she wants a priest. More tests are ordered for tomorrow."

The priest asked if the patient was on the "Seriously Ill (SI)" list—a hospital-wide record of patients that might be reasonably expected to expire within 24 hours. At first I hesitated. She was not on the list. But then, something in me spoke as if the patient was speaking directly to the priest. "Yes, she is." To this day, I do not know why I said this when in actuality her name was not on the list. I had to write her name it on the SI list as I spoke. Was I speaking for the patient? I, later, came to think so.

The priest came in directly. He, too, listened to the patient. That her EKG was normal, her blood pressure was stable and she had no chest pain did not stop his ministry. He understood the patient sought the sustenance scriptures would bring. He fulfilled his role of bringing the word of God to someone who requested it. He opened his old leather-scented Bible and read:

*All my longing lies open before you, Lord.
And my sighing is no secret to you. My heart
throbs, my strength is spent, and the light
has faded from my eyes. The sun will no
longer be your light by day, nor the moon
shine on you by night; the Lord will be your
everlasting light, your God will be your
splendor.*

Isaiah 60:19

The priest brought God's words to the woman. He placed his hand on her forehead and prayed. Her attention was drawn to the empty corner of the room. "Oh, how beautiful," she said. I asked myself, "What was she seeing?" She smiled at me and said, "Thank you," and laid back on the pillows, and slipped into a deep slumber. The pain and suffering on her face were gone.

Enveloped in peace, she slipped away a few hours later despite vigorous resuscitation efforts. Only days later did we learn that the cause of death was a hole that had formed in one of her heart chambers weakened by a heart attack.

We administered CPR. We gave her emergency medications. Nothing helped. Nothing could have facilitated a recovery because the hole allowed blood to collect in the sac around the heart and the heart was squeezed and could not pump blood around as it was meant to do.

Looking back on this time, I believe the priest's visit was ordained to help the woman let go of her earthbound body and journey on to heaven. Was it important that the priest mentioned the light so that when she saw it, she moved unwaveringly toward it, confident it would lead her home? Did she see the light? Putting yourself in her shoes, would you have been reassured by the priest voicing the scriptures?

Ask me who the angel was in this story and I would say the priest who came in the middle of the night offering comfort, giving a blessing…being the light of God… leading someone home.

> Bless the Lord, O you his angels, you mighty ones who do his word, obeying the voice of the world.
>
> Psalm 103:20

This story reinforces the comfort people receive from hearing scriptures when they are dying and is a thanksgiving to all those who bring Bible passages to the bedside of the dying. I rejoiced that these inauspicious circumstances brought the patient peace and love.

Jesus Wants Me

Again Jesus spoke to them, saying, I am the light of the world. Whoever follows me will not walk in darkness, but will have the light of life.

John 8:12

The daughter sat at the bedside of her 84-year-old father when he was called toward the light. He had lived a long life. Lately his days were spent resting in bed fighting to catch his breath. Cancer tumors squeezed his chest making him tired, yet restless. When you cannot breathe, you become anxious and afraid. Your body kicks into high gear. You tire from the constant struggle of gasping for air upon which your life depends.

The daughter said the room smelled like death. Her father's urine was dark with a putrid stench. He ate and drank little. He no longer got up to shower and shook off others' attempts to sponge bathe him. Only God and family saw the man in this condition. He rested in a bedroom that was unobserved far back from the street. It was quiet. His daughter read at his bedside.

After a morning of fitful sleep, the man awoke and sat up in bed although, for many days, he had only been lying down. The man said to his daughter, "Wash me. Jesus is ready for me. I need to be clean." His daughter said her father looked up toward the corner of the room as if he saw something far beyond. Then he laid back down.

Her father's talking about Jesus and heaven caught the daughter by surprise because the man was not a church-going fellow. Yet the man wanted to follow what he heard Jesus say to him. Although he did not attend church regularly, this man, as I understand it from the stories his daughter shared with me, lived the many values taught in the stories of Jesus. He was a railroad engineer who gave up his job so a younger person could have it to care for his growing family. This was a man who saw a crippled child and bought her a walker. He said he had faith she would walk. And she did. This was a man who anonymously gave an elderly mother of a co-worker an electric blanket. He believed the warmth would ease her pain. And it did. These deeds surely are recognized as those of one faithful to the teachings of Jesus. Both in life and in death, the man could see a picture where love— unconditional love—self-sacrificing love— was the putty that bound people together in fellowship of Christian life.

For any person, a father's request to be bathed to be ready to meet Jesus would be a surprise. She asked me if I had ever heard of such talk from a dying person.

I could assure her this cogent talk happens many times. Just when no one expects a dying person to ever utter another word, the dying may sit up and make remarks to family at the bedside that they are being welcomed to another world, they see angels or family, or they have one last piece of advice to give. It is estimated that at least twenty-five percent of such conversations, often documented as hallucinations by doctors and nurses, instead represent edge-of-death conversations the dying are holding with those on the other side.

I told the daughter this story. I was assigned a patient in ICU who was expected to die within hours. He knew it. He told his wife and myself he saw Jesus surrounded by a light. His voice trembled. However, he held on for four hours until each of his children who lived in various parts of the state arrived to say their good-byes. Sons and daughters took their father's hands and said they loved him. When the children were done talking, the dying man made one request to all. "Take care of your mother," he whispered. And, within a half hour of saying these words, his heart stopped. The man was fortunate his body lived on until he completed this mission…an honor and gift to his beloved wife.

So, I could confirm for the daughter whose father said, "Wash me. Jesus is ready for me. I need to be clean," that he saw a being he recognized as Jesus beckoning him. Later that day, in the presence of his daughter, he died. He gave witness to the light and Jesus. He followed his vision of Jesus to heaven.

To further comfort the daughter, I shared a story of a monk who had spent many years steeped in scripture reading. He said to the abbot of the monastery, "I have studied the scriptures. I know all the Psalms by heart. Yet, I do not feel different than when I came to this place. I can recite God's words. Yet I do not feel closer to God." The abbot looked upon the monk, and said, "The point of learning the scriptures is not that you have gone through all the Bible passages." The question is, he said, "Have the stories of the scriptures gone through you? Once they do, you will have found God and Jesus."

So, it was with the man, that the scriptures were working through him as evidenced by the daughter's description of how he helped others.

We know from *John*:

We ourselves are not the light.

John 1:8

Once again Jesus addressed the people:

I am the light of the world. No follower of mine shall walk in darkness; he shall have the light of life.

John 8:12

We can give witness to the light as the old man did. He saw that his Savior wanted him in life and in death. And with that conviction, he asked to be cleansed to be ready to go to heaven.

Jewish Angels

For with you is the fountain of life; in your light we see light.

Psalm 36:9

A middle-aged woman came to talk to me, the Director of Nursing, about her mother. Such a conversation with a daughter was an everyday happening in my role. Family members often had questions about their loved one's condition or treatment plan. Frankly, daughters and sons provided some of the best information about a patient's condition.

The daughter started our talk by saying, "I think something might be wrong with how my mother sees things. My mother has been chattering about seeing angels."

"Walk with me. Let's talk," I said to the daughter. I asked her to tell me what her mother described. "Mom goes down a tunnel toward a bright light. She says she is attracted to the light. Then, mom says angels are sitting on a bench waiting for her. The angels tell mom that she soon will join them in heaven. The angels say they will move over on the bench to make room for her. Mom says the angels are resplendent, gleaming with light."

I asked the daughter if this message was comforting. There was a pause in our conversation as she seemed to turn over in her mind some skepticism. "I guess so," the daughter answered hesitantly. "Though, it's not really part of our religion. We are Jewish. I have been with mom when she sees the angels. She talks to them. And, she is happy doing so. My mother looks up at the corner of the room as if the angels are hovering there. Frankly, while all this talk is going on, I see nothing. I hear nothing. Mom seems unafraid, but she is certain she is going to heaven soon."

I prompted the daughter that in her struggling for an explanation she could look to many readings of the old testament of the Bible that point toward God giving Israelites light. And this light can be interpreted as heaven, a place where we meet God. Because I had been studying the mention of light in the Bible I had this Old Testament Bible passage to share with her:

> *He unveils mysteries deep in obscurity and into thick darkness he brings light.*
>
> *Job 12:22*

I told the daughter that what her mother speaks of is not all that uncommon. At the end of their lives, many patients, talk about seeing a place that others cannot set eyes on just yet. The visions of these people may seem unbelievable to onlookers but are reality to those experiencing them. The veil of life is lifted and dying people are given a preview of what is to come.

There are commonalities in their visions: light, angels, welcoming family and friends. When patients talk about the light of heaven, they describe it as all encompassing, like a hug, making them feel peaceful, secure and loved. The characteristics they describe of the other world are reported by people of all religions.

"So nothing is wrong?" questioned the daughter. I said, "To the contrary, you are telling me your mother is having some experiences that make her happy. She is describing what millions of people talk about before they die. For this, we can feel blessed."

I was able to set up a meeting between the chaplain and the daughter. The daughter came back and told me the chaplain got her interested in reading passages about angels and heaven in the Old Testament. She brought this verse—her favorite– to me.

For God commands the angels to guard you in all your ways.

Psalm 91:11

A Mother as Guide

For you are all children of the light.

1 Thessalonians 5:5

Many times, as a nurse I have come into a room and found a patient talking aloud. I could not see anyone beside the patient from the doorway. And also, upon entering the room, I could find no one inside but the patient. One such day when I was making rounds on patients, I found an elderly woman who was suffering with heart failure.

Patients who are in late stages of heart failure report having trouble catching their breath. Automatically, the muscles in their stomachs stretch to take in air. Patients in extreme heart failure describe feeling overwhelmed by the fluid collecting in airways. And there is nothing they can do to stop it from accumulating. Like in drowning, the fluid prevents air from being exchanged. When there is no oxygen exchange in the lungs, patients become very anxious and restless. They are struggling to breathe.

At 94-years-old and after two heart attacks, Bertha was very tired just from the effort of gulping in air. I put her nasal oxygen prongs back on. I helped her move up in the bed so she could breathe easier. I gently rubbed lotion on her hands.

And then, I saw her open her eyes and heard her speak although not to me. "Mommy, mommy," she called out. "Oh, there you are. You are so beautiful. The light is beautiful." Afterward, Bertha closed her eyes again in sleep while her chest and abdomen moved fast and frantically pushing the oxygen in and out of her lungs. I left the room to get some morphine to calm her and relieve her body's work of breathing.

Later that shift, her family came to the nurses' station. "We think our mother is talking to her mother. But her mother has been dead since she was six-years old. She and her mother were separated when she was a toddler. With the war, her mother went off to find work in the city while Bertha was brought up by aunts in the rural area where she was born.

Bertha's mother labored in a clothing factory. She sent monies home and visited when she could...not often. She was always under pressure to not break thread. Often, the girls and women suffered injuries because they were hungry, cold, and tired. They worked in dimly lit rooms. Bertha's mother ran her machine at great speed working ten-hour days and then collapsed at night in a boarding house where females slept in close quarters—a dozen to a room. She contracted Tuberculosis and died.

Our mother never talked much with us about all this. Our great-aunts told us what happened. Mother kept her feelings to herself. How would our mother remember what her mother looked like when she last saw her as a very young child? Is she hallucinating? This is frustrating all of us. We want to be here for her, but she looks right past us as if we are not in the room."

I wanted to respond to the family's concern of being left out at this emotional end-of-life time. Now that their mother seemed like she was trying to reconnect with her mother, the family seemed to feel rejected. Bertha was in conversation only with her mother. She was not talking to her family who dutifully sat in shifts at the bedside afternoons and evenings. She left family out as she talked to the upper corner of the room where she said she saw a great light and her mother. Bertha's talk with her mother set up a private space around her where her family did not feel welcome.

I explained to the family that as people prepare to die, they make contact with loved ones that already have gone to heaven. A loved one may act as a guide to ease them forward as they shed their earthbound body. The guide may talk back and forth with the ill person for months. And then one day, it happens. The guide leads the patient into the light toward God in heaven. Bertha was experiencing not only the physiological process of dying but also the spiritual side of dying.

The dying person's words often are directed toward their mothers. No one knows why. Conversations of the dying with their mothers do not mean their feelings for those family and loved ones alive and concerned at their bedside are unimportant. Instead, it is apparent that dying persons are present in a zone –a place in time--where we who are alive cannot be. It is as if the curtain between life and death has lifted for them and the dying can see what we cannot. And in this window to heaven, there are beings that were important in their lives. These spiritual beings come to lead the dying across to heaven.

To address the family's surprise that Bertha was now drawn to her mother, I told the family that people often shield their family members from the hurt they have felt in their childhood. Sometimes, the person wants to spare the family pain. Other times, the person may find it easier to put on a persona of "I'm okay. Don't worry about me." as a buffer that neutralizes their own feelings allowing them to go out into the world stronger because they can repress the hurt. Pretending they are all right makes it easier to go on. Bertha may indeed have been traumatized by her mother needing to leave her as a young child, but, stoically, did not speak of her grief. This reconnection with her mother brought Bertha joy as evidenced by the uplifted tone of her voice when talking to her mother. Bertha must have absorbed enough of her mother as a young child to recognize her mother's love now. Love is everlasting.

The family and I discussed how Bertha's talks with her mother did not mean she loved them any less. Families who lovingly take vigil at the dying person's bedside can take heart that the dying patient is not trying to exclude their presence. The person may just be somewhere else temporarily. Being in this "other" zone between life and death does not mean the patient has forgotten them.

It appears from stories of those who have died and returned to life that the presence of family at the bedside may be heard and seen by the dying. So, I encouraged the family to continue to be present to the end of Bertha's life. They would feel good about doing so and Bertha would also be comforted by their presence. Loved ones who learn about death and dying find such knowledge is an experience in consciousness stretching. Family members who recognize the joy of a patient's connection with deceased loved ones develop awareness that there is life beyond life. Families can support the dying person's experience in this space between heaven and earth.

Talks with those with whom we may have unresolved issues may show that life and death is a continuum. Death is not a period, but a comma in the story of life. Death is a transition not a termination. Death is not the end. We all continue to grow up to and through the death event.

This biblical command pulls together what we all saw was happening. Bertha was following the light.

Set your course toward the radiance of the light.

Baruch 4:2

So often, when someone near death talks to people on the other side, that someone is labeled as hallucinating...not being in touch with reality. We need to set the record straight about what really happens at death. Dying people are not hallucinating. Their feet are on earth and their visions are of heaven. Their growth is often being assisted by forces other than their conscious will. Love is part of that eternal existence.

And now these three remain: faith, hope and love. But the greatest of these is love.

1 Corinthians 13:13

The Angel Visit

*For there is nothing hidden that will not be
disclosed, nothing concealed that will not be
made known and brought into the open.*

Luke 8:17

Nurses learn that people who die may stop on
their travel out of their earthbound body to visit in
spirit form ones they love. One of the first times I
heard of a person knowing that someone died even
though there was no rational evidence that the person
should know of the death event was from a hospice
nurse who had worked with dying patients for many
years.

The hospice nurse was at home on her day off
doing household chores -- bent over at the sink

scrubbing some pots and pans--when she recognized the fragrance a patient she was taking care of sprayed on herself each day. The appearance of the scent made the nurse stop what she was doing and think of the patient.

When the nurse arrived back at work the next day, she was not surprised to hear that the patient whose cologne paused her for a moment when she smelled it at home, had died at the same time the scent came to her at home. No one working on the hospice unit thought this a coincidence. These nurses were used to running into spirit forms. They were experienced in how spirits may visit those they love on their way to heaven.

We can draw from the scripture of Luke that there really is nothing hidden at death. Finally, at the end, all is revealed. Luke's words echo a quantum mechanics rationale for what happened. This physics theory recognizes that what happens in one place can be felt at the same time in another place simultaneously, no matter the distance and without a visible connection. In the case of this hospice nurse: There was no discernible thread or force linking the nurse and the patient; the ten-mile distance between the nurse and the hospice, where the death occurred, did not block the transmission; and the death and the nurse knowing of the spiritual visit at death occurred simultaneously.

There are certain events in our lives that seem absolutely real to us but to outside observers may appear to be unbelievable. Sometimes we hesitate to share such experiences with others for fear of others thinking us crazy. Then, a doorway for revealing the happening opens.

A nurse came up to me at a conference after I recounted this story of the hospice nurse visited by the patient as the patient died. She disclosed her experience saying:

"I have hidden this story for a long time. Now, after hearing your talk, I have the guts to talk about it. When my godfather died, he visited me. There, until now, this has been too hard to tell anyone! He was always special to me. John was my hero. He served in the army. Though injured with shrapnel remaining in one leg, he became a baker. He filled the bakery with joviality and wry humor. He was always turning the attention toward customers, trying to make them happy.

I remember how John's eyes filmed over with tears when he told war stories: massive explosions; bodies bloodied and disfigured; moaning quickly followed by fixed, breathless stares; the inability to save the wounded; and orders to move on. He, unwillingly, dragged with him dreadful memories. Unbidden thoughts of death set off his nervous system alarms making him jittery at any sudden sound. He could not hide from the deaths he witnessed. And so, he told me to endure and carry on. He recited a verse an army chaplain had taught him:

For I, the Lord your God, hold your right hand. It is I who say to you, "Fear not, I will help you."

Isaiah 41:13

He said the words, 'I will help you' over and over again. John knew this deliberate repetition brought him strength. He wondered if, in return, he could help others by saying something that would uplift them as the Bible verse had encouraged him.

And that is when he decided to do one good thing, (as he called it), for someone each day…something kind the person did not expect. It could be saying to the squadron cook, 'Great job on that sausage. Was that really meat?' or to the supply clerk, 'I appreciate your keeping things in order. I'm a mess myself.'

John's actions seemed to lessen his haunting dreams of not being able to rescue his buddies in battle. The feeling of always wanting to save them never went entirely away. But, John realized, when you can't save everyone, you can do good in their honor. I believe he came to me as he died as to remind me of this precious teaching that he wished to be passed down.

John said doing a special thing for someone else was not an unselfish act. It was a self-preserving act. Doing one unexpected nice thing for someone did more for him, he said, than it may have done for the person receiving his kindness. *Doing for others helps the doer*, was his mantra.

From the time I was little, he encouraged me to follow his example of giving unexpected kindness. It wasn't hard to get into the habit. I still can remember his smile when he observed me doing one good thing, like complimenting a waitress on doing an exceptional job of serving us. I found it only took a moment to do one good thing but, by doing so, I realized the joy he felt. I also understood that doing one good thing for someone each day made some of my most miserable times better. Even if my life was going downstream on a given day, I could restore someone else's smile.

At the time of my godfather's passing, I was in graduate school. I had three children at home, one of whom was four years old at this time. So, picture this scene. I was trying to write a paper about family functioning while my own brood was making noise and pulling my thoughts away from the task at hand. Luckily, they understood, when I told them, that I needed an hour of quiet.

It was silent in the house. I felt like someone was in the room with me. I stopped writing. Something strange was happening. Although knowing I was alone, I looked around the room...one of those things everyone does when feeling spooked. Thoughts of John came to me. I knew he was not in good health. Living with end-stage emphysema, he moved unsteadily tethered to an oxygen tank. I knew he was in good hands. His wife, Jackie, was a nurse. John and Jackie belonged to a church that sent a Stephen Ministry chaplain once a week to their home. John always took communion praying through Jesus asking for forgiveness of his sins.

This evening, I suddenly came to think of him and all he had done for me over my childhood years. And I reminisced about the one good thing he taught me to do. He was an angel...not just my angel...but someone inspired by a Bible verse on that battlefield to be an angel for others.

My mother called the next day. She said she was the bearer of bad news. My godfather had died. I just listened. I didn't tell her how I was thinking of him--now known to me as at the time of his death. That would have turned the attention toward me. Instead, I considered what one good thing I would do next. In his honor and following his shared wisdom, I am committed to each day being the reason someone smiles."

I thanked the nurse for sharing her story. I think fear of being thought crazy is the reason many who are visited by dying loved ones do not say anything about these stopovers to anyone. A study of widows and widowers revealed that many sensed the visitation of their deceased spouses. People can travel over time and distance to be with loved ones as they depart. If you realize this visiting phenomenon can happen, you may be open to sensing when someone you love stops in on the way to heaven. Then, you will be able to spread the word that the dying—in their spiritual form--can communicate with us as they head to heaven. The spiritual world is open to you if you are willing to believe.

Now, Lord, you are releasing your servant in peace according to your promise. For I have seen with my own eyes the deliverance.

Luke 2:29-30

A Doctor Sees the Light

He was not that light but was sent to bear witness of the light that all men through him might believe.

John 1:8

A physician came up to me at a conference where I had given a talk earlier in the day about my near-death experiences research. He introduced himself, told me his professional background and commented, "I listened to your talk. You've got it right, Sue. I agree with all you said. I saw the light-being who I believe was God." I asked the doctor to tell me more. And, he did. Here is his story.

"I was admitted to the intensive care unit because I collapsed with chest pain. Luckily I was at the hospital. I had not felt well when I awoke that morning. I dismissed my discomfort as indigestion from too much to eat and drink the evening before. I should have connected the dots. I know that people experience more heart attacks early in the morning than any other time of the day. I know that early morning heart attacks are the worst…causing more deaths. But still I let go of my suspicions and went off to work. I am like anyone else who doesn't want to believe what is happening has indeed come to pass. I am a doctor and I should have judged my symptoms worthy of examination.

So I paid the consequences of my shrugging off my fears. I had been walking in the hospital corridor between patient rooms and talking with interns when I collapsed. I was a doctor, but now became the patient—a patient who was dead on the floor—whose heart had stopped.

A resuscitation code was called. There was an outbreak of frenzy. I was suddenly surrounded by a CPR team made up of people I knew. How was I aware of this since I was dead on the floor? I knew because a part of me arose up out of my body and looked down on the scene below. I could see what was going on around my body. I was thinking that I was still the same old me. I would have to describe what I was at that point in time as a spiritual form of myself. I had feelings and thoughts, but my body was on the floor.

When I was out of my body and watching as a spirit from a place near the ceiling as the medical staff performed CPR on me, I felt no physical pain despite staff doing compressions on my chest and zapping me with the defibrillator. I could see that my colleagues were trying hard to resuscitate me.

While the team worked feverishly below me, I felt in no hurry. I was calm. And I was comfortable—free of worries.

Peacefulness like I never experienced before overtook me. I felt united with God. I could see above me an expansive sky. A brilliant, radiant light filled the atmosphere. The light was leading me out of the room away from all the busyness below me. I began to follow it. I was exiting out a top corner of the room leaving the hectic scene of people working over my body below.

A spirit form: This they didn't tell me about in medical school or in my practice as a doctor in a big hospital. I knew patients had spiritual needs but I categorized such things as religious beliefs. I had talks with people facing death when they dropped their masks and told me hush-hush, in private, that they were frightened they might not be good enough at death to go to heaven. Often patients were looking back at their lives and weighing in their minds what they had achieved and how others regarded them. These dying people were taking an inventory to find out if they had become who they intended to be. I found when I listened and didn't interrupt, patients shared their most profound thoughts. These people knew they were dying but they did not believe death ended who they were. Until my own encounter with death, I did not realize that, at these times, patients were really defining their spirit—the part that remained when their body died—the element that was going out of their body on to the next life.

And now, just like the dying patients, I was seeing my spiritual form unfurl. During this CPR episode, when I floated above my body, part of my spirit form was outside and part of it was still inside the room. My wife entered and screamed my name. I looked back down and when I heard her voice cry out my name again and again, I felt a tremendous pull to not leave the room. I wanted to go further along the pathway lit by the light-being, but I found myself popped back into my body in response to her pleading.

Reflection back on this scene and my 40-year experiences as a physician, I took note that none of the doctors with whom I worked ever talked to the patients during CPR. Resuscitation teams discussed the plain facts in front of them---heart rate, heart rhythm, blood pressure, and medication dosages. Orders were barked out at a fast pace. There was no time to spare. Literally, every second counted.

Since this event, I feel that the life I am living is a lesson from God. I believe that at that particular moment — when I was about to leave the room — if my wife had not called me, I would not have returned. I would have followed the light-being. Can someone pleading with a dying patient to stay actually influence life and death? I thought…maybe this could be.

I questioned how I got to this place in life and what I was going to do going forward. I sensed immediately that I am supposed to do something more than being a doctor in this life. My wife's pleading to call me back made me aware that I had been ignoring my responsibilities for making my relationship with my wife work. My long hours immersed in my medical practice were evidence that I thought being a doctor was more important than being an attentive spouse and father. God was saying to me that being a doctor is not the most important thing in the world. Whereas, I thought being a doctor was the highest calling and, therefore the best contribution I could make in this life, now I sensed I was to balance the needs of my patients with the needs of my family. God was telling me that the most important thing in life is to build strong bonds with those I love.

This experience taught me that we are judged by God not by what job we performed in this life, but, rather, how well we relate to those we meet on life's path. That's the message I got from being in the light. I knew immediately I was to take my experience and let it be a light to others in guiding them to focus on relationships not only achievements of this earthly world. My shroud would have no compartments for certificates of accomplishments. My work would be measured in what I left behind with others.

In addition to this lesson, I learned that, when I do emergency procedures on them, my patients might be watching me from a position above, near God. What a joke.

Patients think we doctors are the ones close to God. I learned that patients have both earthbound bodies and spiritual forms. When patients are in the throes of clinical death situations, they may take their spiritual form. Now when I participate in CPR, I wonder, where is the patient's consciousness? Is the patient looking down at their earthly body and me? What is the patient learning during this critical life event? And, I call the patient by name.

In this complex era, people struggle to find out who they are. Many of us do a thousand outstanding things to make a name at work. Excelling can be a compelling aphrodisiac. We take pride in rising to the top. We may equate what we do with who we are. We believe we have controlled our lives. We have been disciplined when others have not and, therefore, we have reaped our just material rewards."

This can be a pitfall the doctor thought.

"This incident has taught me that I am no different than any other person at the end of life. We are all bodies and spirits. We are all going on a journey toward the light.

As a doctor, I am not just my brother's keeper as I maintain the Hippocratic Oath. I may have appeared different than my brother in life. But, in death, I am just like my brother."

Unless people have made time for relationships with God in their lives, after careers are over, they may struggle for day-to-day meaning. The money they thought counted, doesn't count. The homes and the cars they own only show they know how to make and use money. They may ask themselves what counts in the end. The doctor asked himself, "What can I do to best help others understand what I have learned really happens at death?" And, his answer was to tell his story.

> Let your light so shine before men, that they may see your good works, and glorify your Father who is in heaven.
>
> *Matthew 5:1*

Time to Go to Heaven

The people that have lived in darkness have seen great light. Light has shined on those who lived in the land of death's dark shadow.

Matthew 4:16

Theresa had multiple myeloma. She had survived three years since diagnosis. Inside her body, cells were proliferating, knocking out the proper functioning of her kidneys and taking over the inside of her bones causing severe pain and debility.

Physically, Theresa was tired and weak from coping with a myriad of symptoms including a series of infections, one of which landed her in the hospital this time. Emotionally, she was trying her best to cope with leaving two young children in the care of relatives and friends while she was in the hospital.

Hospitalizations were becoming more frequent with smaller time spans between each. Acquaintances paid their respects. Visitors did not stay long. The withered look of her body and the tortured face of her husband made people anxious. Intellectually, Theresa and her husband knew she would not recover. They held hands in silence, encircled by a private space that allowed each to grapple with their own feelings and fears while still being close. The shared quiet was more comfortable than words could be.

When outside the hospital room, Theresa's husband prayed aloud to God. His words were those of a man desperate to hold onto one he loved. He railed against God. "How can you? Why her? She loves you. Why should she suffer? No one should be called God who looks down on her suffering and does nothing. I will give up anything if you let her live." But, as the darkness of each night fell, tears trickled down his face and he got down on his knees at Theresa's bedside and prayed for a miracle.

We—her friends—also knew she was dying. Theresa was our colleague. We all taught nursing in a Catholic school of nursing. So that is why we could see what we didn't like the look of—what was going to happen down the road as the multiple myeloma progressed. Nurses find it very hard when one of our own has cancer. We feel so helpless because we are by nature people who want to help those who cannot help themselves.

We all knew that there was nothing we could do to prolong Theresa's life. The disease had disrupted nature and the disease would take its course. We could only hope to help Theresa be safe and comfortable. We all agreed that our best option would be to listen to Theresa and carry out her wishes. So we took turns at her bedside doing this.

We fluffed her pillow. We helped her sip juice. We gently rubbed lotion on her skin. We let her lean on us when she still could walk to the bathroom. We were her voice to the nurses when she was too tired or nauseous to ask for more medication. We brought her children for visits.

Theresa made sure life outside the hospital went on for her girls. She arranged playdates for them in the neighborhood.

Theresa pulled herself together to be strong when her eight and twelve-year-old daughters came to see her. Her cheeriness masked the desperation she must have felt knowing her hugging them might be her last touch. Memories and love were all she could take with her. Parents say death of a child is the most excruciating pain one can experience. By her own death, Theresa was losing her children too. Placing her hand over her heart, she told the girls, "You will always have me in here." The power of her love astounded me.

Darla whose thirteenth birthday was five days away was looking forward to a skating party with friends. "You won't die on my birthday, mama," she pleaded. Theresa said assuredly, "No, Darla, I won't."

Looking on, I wondered how she could make such a promise. As a nurse, I witnessed death grasping patients unexpectedly. But I said nothing. So often mothers reassure their children when such support can best be characterized as hope rather than real knowledge of what is to come. It just felt so not right these girls were soon to be motherless.

In her weakened condition, Theresa slept quietly most of the time this last hospitalization. So it surprised those of us sitting in her room when she sat straight up in bed and began to talk. She directed her voice to the ceiling in the corner of the hospital room. We could not see anyone in the corner. Her words were clear. Theresa said, "I am ready. I see the horsemen and the carriage of angels. I see the light toward heaven. I am coming."

Theresa told those of us present that she said she was getting ready to go to heaven and four horsemen had come to guide her. Theresa told us she saw a radiant light that marked the path toward heaven. She said she was ready to die.

The look on Theresa's face was one of wonder. Sadness left her. She did not appear apprehensive. On the contrary, she looked at ease. She talked about the bright light making her feel loved. The light forecasted in the verse of Matthew shined on her as death met her. Then, she lay down in bed and folded herself into her husband's arms. Within minutes, he watched her slip from this world to the next. It was the day before her daughter's birthday. She kept her promise.

Theresa gave us a great gift. She shared her view of heaven. We all whispered a prayer of thanksgiving for the lesson about life and death that Theresa confirmed for us. Then we sat in quiet, comforted by each other's presence as we processed individually all we had witnessed.

Later, we watched as Theresa's husband told the girls their mother was resting in heaven. As he held them snuggly in his arms, he said, "You are my angels here and your mother is our angel in heaven."

Like the lamp, you must shed light among your fellows, so that, when they see the good you do, they may give praise to your Father in Heaven.

Matthew 5:16

A Daughter Lighting the Pathway to Heaven

Arise, shine, for your light has come, and the glory of the Lord has risen upon you.

Isaiah 45:7

As a Director of Nursing in a nursing home, every minute passes quickly. There is more paperwork to do than can be reasonably done in an eight-hour day. In order to get a break and recharge my battery on what was really important, I would go see the people who lived there and their families. This story is about a time like that.

As I walked by Sara, a patient who was 100 years old, I smiled at her. She stretched out her hand.

I took it in mine and crouched down by the side of her wheelchair to chat. I was going to a seminar out of town for a couple days and would be leaving for the airport in a few hours. Sara said, "Will you miss me if I'm gone when you come back? I'm going to miss you."

I replied to Sara asking why she was hinting she might be gone. I said, "Tell me, Sara, why do you think you will not be here when I get back?" Sara told me that she had seen her daughter recently. Her response would not be significant had not her daughter died many years before. I remembered the reason Sara was admitted to the nursing home was because she had nowhere else to go and get the day-to-day help she needed when her daughter passed on.

Sara had not talked of her daughter to me since I asked her background questions at admission to the nursing home ten years ago. She seemed to have pushed such memories deep down. It was complicated. I knew from our initial conversation that Sara was ashamed of the indignity of the circumstances of her daughter's death. Her daughter died after prolonged illegal drug use, interwoven within her lifestyle choice to live with men who abused her.

Sara's shame stemmed from the fact that her husband had not been a proper father to her daughter. Sara's husband had been born into a family whose preceding generation could produce no daughters, making all the brothers desire daughters not sons. Her husband was the only boy cousin. All his uncles had succeeded in producing much preferred daughters. He couldn't escape his own jealously of his sisters receiving greater attention from his parents than he. Whenever he saw his daughter cradled in Sara's arms, his resentment stirred up anger which he took out on the child, first verbally and then physically, as she grew up. A father's relationship has a deep effect on a daughter's association with men. Sara knew her daughter paid for her father's insecurity and envy.

But now Sara's voice expressed a happiness.

"My daughter told me she has two chairs in heaven and one is for me. I will be joining her soon. She told me it is so beautiful in heaven. There is a light and there is love everywhere. Everyone is loved. My daughter looked beautiful like an angel. I did not see wings but she had on a wonderful, flowing dress. My daughter was sitting on one of the chairs.

She pointed at the other. She said I should be ready to go soon. I do not think I will reach 101. My birthday is next week. God will take me to heaven before then."

My experiences with patients had shown me that Sara could be right. As people approach the threshold of death, the previously impermeable barrier between this life and the next can dissolve. Unexpectedly, the person may glimpse a new reality. It sounded like Sara was able to communicate with her daughter in heaven and was being prepared for her journey. I heard many patients talking to loved ones who had died. Her daughter was bearing witness to the light in heaven. Patients who have been over to the other side and back, talk about the light drawing them toward heaven. They say the light was like a being that gave them unconditional love. So Sara's story was in sync with others I had heard.

Yet, I also knew from experience that some patients talked to others in heaven for weeks and months before they died. So, I did not say my good-bye. I did tell Sara I was happy she had conversations with her daughter. I did confirm for Sara that people do talk with loved ones who have died and that these loved ones often welcome them into heaven.

When I returned from the seminar days later, Sara was still alive. She did not seem unhappy that she had not yet died for she was enjoying her continued conversations with her daughter and reasonably good health. Serendipitously, she had gained some fame amongst her peers as she related her visions of heaven to groups of other residents of the nursing home. Most had not even known Sara had a daughter. But, they were pleased for her. And, her story brought many people comfort because it showed a mother's and daughter's love endured forever no matter what the narrative of their earthly lives. Sara persisted in saying she did not have long to live because her chair in heaven was ready for her.

Sara continued conversations with her daughter until she died six months after her 101st birthday. When her health failed, staff members observed Sara talking more frequently to her daughter. The last word that left her lips was her daughter's name. Sara was laid to rest wearing an outfit she chose—an embroidered blouse made by the fine skills of her daughter.

The nursing home Bible study group talked about Sara, her vision and her conversations with her deceased daughter. All agreed that Sara's daughter had lit the path toward heaven. In honor of the daughter's loving presence in her mother's life, the chaplain had this scripture engraved on a memorial plaque for Sara:

Send forth your light and your truth so they may guide me.

Psalm 43:3

Reach Toward the Light

*But if we walk in the light as He is in the
light, we have fellowship with one another,
and the blood of Jesus his Son cleanses us
from all sin.*

John 1:17

Joey was a muscle-bodied young man in his
early twenties. He was fit from routine hours at the
gym after his work on the assembly line making auto
parts. He drove a vintage Mustang. The high school
kids in the neighborhood looked up to him. That is
why it was so easy to sell them a little weed.

He'd served some jail time for drug peddling. Not a model prisoner, he often was in solitary confinement, (the hole), for infractions…usually nudging another prisoner who then shot a punch back. Joey said he couldn't resist a fist fight. He knew he was good at boxing. He liked a brawl.

They say you have to make a decision in prison to continue to act as hostile as you did on the outside or to go deeper into your core and pull out whatever reserve you have to become disciplined in carrying out the behaviors of the good inmate. Being a model prisoner buys you privileges: Access to the internet, visits by family and friends, and the opportunity for education. Displays of anger bury you deeper into social systems used by guards and other inmates to control those they see as bucking their systems.

I heard of a young man who chose being in "the hole" for some practical reasons. In solitary confinement, no one could harass him. So he'd incite the guards to get thrown in and, for a time, be in a place where he could hear himself think. He could cry and no one saw or heard him. Solitary confinement became a safe place where he could get in touch with who he was and who he wanted to be.

When imprisoned on Robbins Island, Nelson Mandela made a choice to become someone he was not when he entered the jail confines. Mandela had been an angry man. He was labeled a terrorist because he had led forces that attacked the government. In jail, he stifled his rage because it didn't get him or his cause anywhere. He negotiated. He compromised his principles saying some principles cost too much. Mandela practiced self-discipline—a way of being that served him and his anti-apartheid cause very well.

But, Joey was excitable…bouncing off the walls. He did not have the self-control to tamp down his day-to-day troubling emotions. His behavior became more aggressive as the moon waxed—a sign of mental fragility. He was not able to act calm even though composure might have influenced the treatment he experienced at the hands of guards. Expressing his anger in prison came at great cost. After a turbulent incarceration, he emerged a resentful young man, easy to rile and blind to his own shortcomings, blaming others for his lot in life.

So it was no surprise when he continued selling drugs and ran into trouble often. After being beat up by members of a rival gang, he noticed some weakness in his legs but shook it off. Then he started losing his balance, missing a strike or two at the punching bag at the gym. Being inadequate did not go along with his temperament. So he pushed himself harder at the gym. Then one day, other boxers had to pick him up off the floor. Joey could not get up on his own accord.

A work-up at his local hospital showed Joey had a tumor encircling his spinal cord. Surgeons tried to remove the entire mass but the numbness and weakness he was feeling in his legs worked its way into paralysis. Joey's fight to go on dwindled in the hospital. He was not eating much and not interested in talking with other patients or staff. He developed pneumonia and wanted to sleep all the time. Sleep can be a place people go so they don't have to think and feel. He slept many days away.

This young man entered the nursing home where I was *Director of Nursing* because the hospital could do no more for him, and his daily needs could not be met at home where family had given up on having a relationship with him. When Joey arrived, his expression was vacant. He did not make eye contact with the nurses and nursing assistants. It was as though he was looking straight through them, treating them as nonexistent. The internal torment of his imprisonment could not be buried. He grunted replies. He picked at the food on his tray. His illness not only changed him visibly but also had hidden him in a curtained off place where he did not allow others entrance.

A physical therapist exercised his arms and legs to keep muscle tone. Occupational therapists splinted his hands to prevent contractures. Nursing assistants bathed, fed and clothed him. And Joey retreated more and more into himself making heated remarks under his breath, blaming the world for his troubles.

Nursing home staff would hear Joey screaming when his dreams turned into nightmares. In his dreams, he moved in and out of the present and past. His whimpers in the night were interrupted by his screaming. In dream, he slipped into a narrative he could not leave behind. Joey imagined he was facing gang members slamming him against walls in his room. He would imagine bleeding —lots of it, teeth dropping to the floor. He tried to fight back but kept missing. His punches landed in the spaces between people. He couldn't defend himself. He was frightened. His night terrors covered a complicated accumulation of feelings. As he awoke, he realized he was again all alone. And being all alone was upsetting too. Joey's dreams were his private landscapes where nurses could not follow.

Although, nursing staff members talked and joked with Joey, he did not reveal much about his thoughts. He tried to close his feelings to staff and family. He was thinking that if these people mean nothing to me, I do not need them. Later, he would say he always was hiding tears that never seemed very far away. His face registered a somber expression. His loneliness was carved upon it like a mask. Sensing he could not break into Joey's isolation, a nursing assistant sought the assistance of a social worker.

At the encouragement of the nursing home's social worker, Joey's family began to visit. Everyone seemed weighted down by their past history with Joey. Joey's mother confided in me she kept thinking she could change him. She'd rescue him from one bad situation only to find herself bailing him out of another. Years of her life were consumed with angst about his. She never told the others her last conversation with Joey was when he said to butt out of his life. He yelled that he never wanted to see her again if she wouldn't stop asking him questions about what he was doing. "I pretended this talk didn't happen because I was so humiliated," she revealed. I could understand the detachment she displayed now. Her son seemed determined to drive her away. I told her she need not be embarrassed. Nurses often see families that have drifted apart come back together when a family member is ill. I let her know, "Sometimes you cannot save a person you love. You have to step back and save yourself." I made a habit of bringing her cups of tea as a way of gesturing opportunities to spend time talking with me. I was hoping—even without words—to bring her comfort.

At first the family wore their scorn for Joey's drug use on their faces. Their postures—not making eye contact and standing with arms crossed over their chests demonstrated their detachment. His prison time disrupted their lives and made them ashamed.

Then, a physical therapist took one brother's hand and coached him to massage Joey's calf muscle to relieve the pain of spasms. Nursing assistants showed family members how to put lotion on Joey's dry skin. Their touching Joey was the beginning of communication.

Staff members thought it a great day when his mother and brothers voiced they understood that Joey, like all of us, had made some mistakes of foolishness. They said they realized Joey's slip-ups had bigger consequences than may have been warranted. They realized that incarceration did not help Joey. It hardened him.

Months passed and Joey's mother and brothers shared stories about when Joey was a young child. Family joined staff members in talking with Joey about his love of boxing. A brother brought in a framed photo of Joey in the ring. Joey showed he began to care about family members, asking nurses when they would next visit. This was a sign of Joey changing. Who we care about and want to spend time with tell us a great deal about who we are. He was growing away from his narcissistic self and beginning to show an appreciation for his family. He was beginning to realize everyone needs people. Joey's mother and brothers told him they loved him.

Joey was raised in a large Lutheran family and the nursing home was a Lutheran facility that covered the expenses of patients in need, like Joey. There were a few nondenominational chaplains that visited patients like Joey who did not have membership in a church.

Chaplains would ask nurses who might welcome some talk and prayer. A nurse described Joey as a difficult young man who pushed others away. One chaplain was not dissuaded. His own youth had been filled with impatience and disillusionment. He went into Joey's room with a personal understanding of how a troubled adolescence could leave a scar on a young man. He was just the person to dismantle Joey's remoteness. The chaplain knew about boxing so their first talks were about their shared love of the sport. They talked about the great ones—Joe Frazier and Rocky Marciano—Joey's heroes. Such conversation segued into thoughts about death and meeting people, such as these champions, in heaven. The chaplain explained to Joey about praying for forgiveness through Jesus. And they did so.

Joey shared his boxing stories and dreams for success in the ring. He allowed his fear of revealing himself to unravel. Nurses were grateful for the chaplain's ability to talk with Joey about his unsettling nightmares. Joey boasted to the chaplain, "I am on the fast track to heaven." He told the nursing assistants, "Here today, heaven tomorrow. We all have to go sometime. I am ready to meet my maker's angry face. I can explain it all." His outbursts seemed to show he was trying to seek affirmation that heaven was real and that he, after some drug busts, street fights and jail time, would be forgiven by God.

As his weakness and discomfort worsened, Joey told the visiting chaplain he did not want to live. He was fuming at circumstances that put him in "a chair" for the rest of his life. And, he told others the same thing by not cooperating with caregivers and refusing to eat. He talked less. He began to be adrift in his own thoughts for long periods. He lost weight but refused nutritional support measures. His heart started beating in an irregular pattern. His physician warned Joey of the possible consequences of not accepting medications.

Joey was in an angry place with fresh worry about God. Would God be mad? Would God be forgiving? The chaplain explained to Joey that God would know what he had done. And, despite it all, God would forgive. The chaplain also said the parables of Jesus teach us to forgive others. He asked Joey to consider forgiving the gang members who hurt him. That advice only brought screams of defiance. "I will never forgive them," Joey said. As often in his life, he blamed those in the other gang and characterized himself as a victim, which was not, in fact, always reality.

But, Joey's family was getting tired, for they had families of their own to care for and lives that also demanded their time. When Joey's weight dropped dramatically, and he looked skeletal, they asked me how long he had to live. I said, "Only God knows." They stared ahead exhausted but continued their vigil. I believed Joey was aware of their weariness. Yet, he also did not want to be alone. He wanted family beside him.

Then, one morning Joey brightened. He talked with a young male nursing assistant about a new and surprising experience he had during the night when he was in unrelenting pain. He found himself "popped" out of his body and, from a spot above, could see himself in bed. Joey told the nursing assistant he took the involuntary trip out of his body down a tunnel toward a bright light that seemed to be beckoning him. A voice said, "Do not be afraid." Joey wasn't. "I loved being in this deep zone," he reported. "I was bone tired from hurting, but in the tunnel, I felt light and pain free. I don't know how it happened."

Joey told the young man that he began to understand he was more than a body. He realized he still existed without his physical body. It was fortunate the young nursing assistant had knowledge of how the dying may separate from their bodies near the end of their lives. He was able to reassure Joey that he was not only a body but also a spirit form that lived on no matter how sick the body became. The nursing assistant reported the conversation to me. It seemed Joey was witnessing the pathway to heaven.

Once when his family took a dinner break, I let Joey know that I could see his family loved him very much. I also made Joey aware that family members understood he was dying. I told Joey what I had learned from dying patients—that a bright light would come to him—a light people described as a loving being. I explained he could follow the light down a tunnel to heaven. Light has long been connected with a pathway to heaven. Ancient recordings say lightning is the finger of God.

"It is okay to leave when you are ready. Your family will be alright," I said. I told Joey his family was happy that he began to show love for them and they would carry his love with them always. I said, "Joey, you will be okay, for God loves everyone."

Joey whispered he wanted his family to stay with him until the end. "Please," he said, "'til the end."

An evening later I stopped into Joey's room just to say good-bye for the day. His mother and brothers were there. Joey was taking shallow and slow breaths. In the stillness, there was a sense of calm. My intuition told me Joey's spirit was leaving. Family asked me if I thought death would come soon. I told them I never knew for sure. I offered to call the chaplain.

The chaplain had a short talk with Joey before Joey gave up this life. Close by Joey's pillow, he read this scripture:

> *This is the message we have heard from him and proclaim to you, that God is light, and in him is no darkness at all.*
>
> *John 1:15*

Family members openly shared their love for Joey. Each said their good-byes. I believe Joey's spirit stayed there long enough to see and hear his family say they would see him again in heaven.

I stayed with the family for a while at the bedside. "I thought I'd feel sadder," Joey's mother confided. "I was angry with him for so long. Now I am happy he is at peace where he knows he needn't be afraid anymore."

Did I believe that what the chaplain and I told Joey made him know he would be okay when he died? Yes. Do I believe that in sharing that God forgives and that a bright light will welcome a patient into heaven may augment patient's readiness to die? Yes, indeed. That's how death works.

Was Joey finally able to let go of the boy who used bravado to hide his feelings? Had that young, anxious man died and a new man who could look ahead born? Life is most importantly about relationships. They strengthen us and bring us a better picture of who we really are. Joey went forth reconciled, forgiven and strong.

But because of his great love for us, God, who is rich in mercy, made us alive with Christ even when we were dead in transgressions. It is by grace you have been saved.

Ephesians 2:4-5

The Grace of God

*Let us open our eyes to the light that comes
from God, and our ears to the voice from the
heavens that every day calls out this charge:
If you hear God's voice today, do not harden
your hearts.*

Psalm 95:8

It was a Saturday. I received a call from the
receptionist at a Catholic nursing home where I was
Director of Nursing. A priest was requesting
admission for an 89-year-old woman whose niece had
been active in his congregation. The niece faced an
unsettling day. Her dying mother was being
transferred from the hospital to an in-patient hospice
house. At the same time, her aunt, who also was

about to die, was being discharged from the hospital with nowhere to go.

Hospital social workers had been unable to find placement of the aunt for a couple reasons. Facilities were refusing to take the aunt because she would likely die soon after admission. The patient would require hours and hours of admission assessment and paperwork which translated into time and salary for nurses for very little long-term payout in days of patient stay.

The priest had the receptionist call me because he knew the niece and wanted to help her by accepting the aunt for placement in our nursing home. I said I would come into the nursing home and take care of the details. Approval of the transfer fit the mission of the Catholic community that ran the nursing home. The sisters would not back off from helping because the admission would not be profitable. I just had to make it happen.

My first thought was to place the aunt on a nursing unit that was calm that day. A private room was not available anywhere in the facility. I rounded on all the units talking with nurses about the anticipated intensity of their work in the next 24 hours. I was seeking a quiet space where the staff was not too rushed so there would be time for them to frequently interact with the new resident. With the niece also needing to be with her mother at a hospice down the road, staff would be called on to be the family for this new resident.

After talking with the assigned hospital social worker, I asked that physician orders for care be faxed over. The woman was on hospice care which meant only the procedures essential to her comfort were prescribed. I had to make sure we were following these orders. But I also knew we had to be following the patient's wishes. We had to figure out not just what the patient required but also what the person wanted. The hospital records indicated the woman was non-communicative, unresponsive to voice instructions, and totally dependent on staff for eating, drinking, and moving in bed. The physician orders were morphine sulfate drops for comfort and to relax breathing and scopolamine to dry up annoying secretions (fluids) in the patient's throat and windpipe. These were typical comfort care measures.

The patient was unable to say what she wanted. So next, I phoned the niece, first extending concern for her situation and secondly, telling her we would help all we could. The niece wished to swing by the nursing home to see her aunt and then, go on to join her mother in her final moments. We agreed I would call the niece when her aunt arrived at our place.

"Oh, but for the grace of God," was the thought that went through my mind as I saw the woman being lifted off the transport cart and into bed. The room was clear of other residents who lived in the room. And there she was…hair matted, dried secretions around her eyes and mouth, food scraps stuck in gaps between her teeth, and dry, flaking skin. The sleeve of her hospital gown slipped down revealing her emaciated form. Neck veins protruded. Breath sounds gurgled. Her stomach rose with each breath as abdominal muscles help push air in and out of her lungs. Her breaths were irregular…interrupted with gasps and moaning.

I don't know if it really matters except to the outside world how we look when we pass over. I have an idea of the patient's perspective. Stories of those hovering between life and death when their hearts stopped indicated that the person's bodily appearance was of no importance to them as death neared. I asked myself to whom then did it matter? To whom should it matter? All these questions flowed into one query: What do I do now?

I was concerned the niece would feel awful when she saw her aunt in this disheveled condition. Quickly, I enlisted the help of a kindhearted, hard-working nursing assistant experienced in the care of someone dying. We got some warm water and washed away the debris from the patient's face. With much patience and persistence, we brushed the tangles out of the patient's hair and combed it nicely around her face. The nursing assistant carefully cleaned her teeth and I suctioned the fluids out of the pockets of her mouth. When we rolled her side to side, she moaned. I administered morphine drops. Positioning the woman with her head elevated allowed secretions to flow by gravity downward. The gurgling stopped. We placed rolled up blankets at the side of her body supporting her in a sitting position. Because of these measures, the patient no longer gasped for breath. She sighed but no longer groaned.

During the performance of all these hygiene procedures, we chatted in one-sided conversation with the woman. This nursing assistant had met me at another bedside a previous time when a unit nurse had come for me to verify a patient was indeed dead.

That day the nursing assistant saw me greet the dead patient reminding her who I was and why I was at her side. On this occasion, after cares were completed, I had debriefed the nursing assistant telling her the reason behind my actions. Talking to the dead may shock some people until they understand that patients who have gone over to the other side and back report that they could see and hear what was happening around their bodies when they were clinically dead. My dialogue was in response to this phenomenon.

So, because of the nursing assistant's knowledge of the reports of people who had near-death experiences, she easily fell into the conversation with this woman who was very near death. We let the woman know we cared about how she felt and were trying to make her as comfortable as possible. We told her that her niece would be coming, and we wanted to make her look and feel her best for that visit.

By observation, we could tell we succeeded in improving the woman's comfort and appearance because when the niece came in, at first sight of her aunt, she touched her palm to her chest, took a deep breath, and, with tears welling in her eyes, said, "My aunt looks so much happier here." It mattered to her. I know it mattered to the nursing assistant and me too.

The niece sat down in a chair at the bedside and stroked her aunt's hand. I left the room hearing her say, "Let me tell you how much you meant to me as I grew up. I want you to know I love you and mom loves you."

When I checked back, I saw the niece rubbing her knuckles over her eyes, obviously tired, trying to bridge the two worlds of responsibility for end-of-life care for both her mother and aunt. She was carrying so much grief. I imagined she was reluctant to leave yet also drawn by her mother's grave condition, to go.

I presumed from sentiments of the niece's I overheard, that she and her aunt had a close friendship and history. I asked if the niece would like to tape record a message to be played at her aunt's bedside. In the past, I found such recordings comforting not only for the dying crossing over but also for family members who could not stay at the bedside of the loved one.

And so the niece spoke what well could be her last words to her aunt into a recorder that I placed on the bedside table. By leaving her presence on the tape for nurses to play from time to time, I hoped letting go was made a bit easier for the niece. Death is one of many life journeys. The niece's message could frame her aunt's final one.

I asked the niece if there was anything else we could do in her absence. The niece said, "Really, you are doing so much." "Yes, really. We want to do all we can to help," I replied. The niece mentioned that her aunt went to mass almost daily until the spell of illness that led to this hospitalization. She shrugged her shoulders exclaiming this would not be possible. I inquired if the aunt had favorite Bible verses from these services. The niece said that her aunt much loved the Psalms.

I requested a Catholic volunteer who was especially knowledgeable of scripture to sit beside the aunt and read Psalms. The niece and I stayed with the volunteer for a time. Her words flowed melodiously. The volunteer knew she was speaking to someone who could hear her. God's word reached the woman through the volunteer.

Bless the Lord, my soul. Lord my God, you are very great. Clothed in majesty and splendor and enfolded in a robe of light.

Psalm 104:1-2

Your word is revealed, and all is light; it gives understanding even to the untaught.

Psalm 119:130

The niece watched for a while and then, not quite as sad as when she arrived at her aunt's side, tiptoed out of the room. She could move forward knowing she had done the best she could in these circumstances, and her aunt was in good hands.

The aunt moved in and out of consciousness probably hearing and seeing what was going on around her bed. After a time, her breathing calmed and her chest rose and sank smoothly. The priest came and blessed her. God's voice and her niece's recorded message played at the bedside met her as she began her journey home.

Someday each of us will wonder what we have spent our lives doing. Some things we do for others, although not significant in terms of our time and effort, are immeasurable in the quality of what the other person gains. But, each thing we do for others can teach us who we are. Spending the end of life with a person who needs us can be the beginning of a new awareness of our mission in life.

In responding to the niece's request for someone to read scriptures, the volunteer found within her the power of God that is in each of us. She said, "Reading scriptures as death came made me truly understand how sharing my Christian religion could make a difference in someone's life." The volunteer missed the noon mass service she regularly attended but made her religion genuine through spending this time with the dying woman. D.H. Lawrence in his poem "We are Transmitters," wrote, "And if, as we work, we can transmit life into our work, life, still more life, rushes into us...and we ripple with life through the days. Give and it shall be given unto you." I came to understand this volunteer was an angel sent forth from God. She played a significant role in this patient's calm crossover into heaven. The volunteer practiced her religion authentically.

By God's grace, I am what I am.

I Corinthians 15:10

Let your light so shine before men, that they may see your good works, and glorify your Father which is in heaven.

Matthew 5:16

Let the Little Children Come Unto Me

Let the children come to me; do not hinder them, for to such belongs the kingdom of God.

Mark 10:13-14

We can make an effort to comprehend someone else's tragedy. When a grieving person cries, we struggle to find words to respond. We say, "I'm sorry for your loss" in order to communicate that we are terribly sad we cannot erase away the death. Once you have yourself lost a loved one, you can better identify with the person staring out blankly from beneath tears. When you've been there, you understand what it is like to have your mind be frozen in time, way out there on an invisible ice flow, and your attention only partly present to people in your everyday life. People walk by and you do not look at them or care. You stare out stuck in the freshly wet, slippery, sticky, mud of your grief.

Nothing hurts as much as the loss of a child. You can witness the pain of those whose children die. But unlike other deaths, I am not sure you can truly feel the depth of hurt of such loss unless it happens to you.

The death of a child is not truly comprehensible to those of us spared. But that does not mean we cannot learn from the stories of parents who grieve and the children who go over to the other side and return to tell their stories of heaven. We can comfort those parents who have lost children when we know stories critically ill children tell us.

As a clinical nurse specialist, I was asked to meet with a father who had been called to the hospital where his family was taken after a car accident. His wife was being treated in surgery. He had not spoken with her. One son had died. Another son was sedated and now asleep but expected to fully recover. Life for this family, like many, was not following the path they had envisioned. For this family, everything changed. Their future life was snatched away in one fatal, unfortunate moment.

The mother was driving when the accident happened. The highway was snow packed and visibility was poor. Two boys, ages four and six, were strapped in car seats in the backseat. A truck plowed into the side of the car killing the four-year-old and severely injuring the mother. The six-year-old suffered "minor injuries".

I found the father pacing back and forth in a hospital corridor outside the operating room. He was awaiting news about his wife. I introduced myself and we sat down in an unoccupied alcove. His head hung low over his chest and he wrung his hands again and again, dropping his phone more than once. Disbelief hung like heavy gray fog in the air between us. It had been only six hours since the accident. His life was unexpectedly unspooling.

I said, "I am a nurse. I can sit with you while you wait. We can talk if and when you want." The man shrugged his shoulders.

I took this response as, "I don't know. I don't care. I don't even get what is happening." I explained

I had a report from the operating room that things were going well. I asked if I could help him make calls to family or friends. "Oh," he said as if suddenly drawn back into the world outside his inner thoughts, "Yes, I cannot seem to find the right numbers." Most times the best thing you can do for people in shock after the loss of a loved one is to say, "Tell me, what I can do for you right now," and follow their lead. One by one, as he directed, I punched in the person's name on the contact list and then handed him back the phone so he could relay the bad news to the people on the other end of the line.

"It can't be. Just can't be," the father sobbed. "How can Joseph be gone? I can't believe it. I hugged him this morning. Have you seen him? Have you seen him dead?" I told the father I could arrange for us to see Joseph. I told him he could hold his son who died. Our hospital had a protocol that supported this physical contact of a parent with a child who died. This practice often made deaths more believable for parents. I left the father with some water and a promise I would return as soon as I could make arrangements for him to be with his son.

A half hour later, I led the father into a sparsely furnished room where the child's body had been wrapped in a blanket and placed in a crib. A bandage hid the top of the child's head, but some bruising, puffiness and lacerations were visible on the child's pale, sunken face. His broken limbs were swaddled tightly by the blanket. A chaplain joined us offering condolences and looking for a path down which to proceed. After finding out the father's religion was Christian, the chaplain led us in prayer as we three looked down at the child. The chaplain quoted Jesus saying:

> *Whoever welcomes one of these little children in my name welcomes me.*
>
> *Mark 9:36-37*

"Where is he? Where is he really?" the father asked. The chaplain assured us that the child and all children were welcomed into heaven. "But won't he be scared without us?" the father cried. "He's all alone." The chaplain said scripture taught:

In my Father's house are many rooms. If it were not so, would I have told you that I go to prepare a place for you? And if I go and prepare a place for you, I will come again and will take you to myself, that where I am you may be also.

John 14:2-3

It is beyond any parent's imagination to picture their child on their own somewhere out there where the parent cannot reach them. But, I knew a story a child told about her visit to heaven. I thought it a comforting story and now was the time to share it with a parent who sought to grasp where his child was.

I began by saying children have told us some consistent things about dying and heaven. Nurses and doctors have talked to many critically sick children who have near-death experiences wherein they leave their bodies and travel onward to heaven and back. I recounted the story of a girl of ten who had come from a small town in another country to a big university hospital in hope of being cured of a cancer untreatable elsewhere. The girl, Erin, went through rounds of chemotherapy. This treatment— given over many months, did not arrest the cancer. A sister provided bone marrow for a transplant. Erin's body did not respond favorably. Her condition worsened. She became uncomfortable and exhausted. She was restricted to an isolation cubicle in the pediatric intensive care unit. Only doctors, nurses, family, a pastor and her best friend, Molly, were allowed to visit because the risk for Erin picking up an infection from germs others brought in was great.

One afternoon, Erin requested the nurse to call her friend, Molly, and ask her to visit. Molly's mother brought her to the ICU early in the afternoon. Molly washed her hands, put on gown, gloves and a mask and a surgical hat to protect Erin from microbes. The girls laughed at the sight of Molly with only her glasses peering out of all the protective hospital paraphernalia. Molly pointed at Erin with the limp ends of the fingers of the gloves too big for her, and said, "Don't you laugh at me!" But, they both giggled hysterically.

The girls talked about their brothers. Molly told Erin the boys made a snow fort on a hill in the courtyard and it collapsed on them sending them scrambling for their lives. Erin and Molly howled envisioning the sight of the boys being afraid and digging their way out.

Then Erin's voice turned serious. She told Molly, "You know I've been on a trip through a tunnel and I sat on Jesus' lap. He told me not to be afraid. It was just like Pastor Dean said Jesus is. He was so nice. Jesus said I can go be with Him. I want to go. I am tired." Erin said she felt good when visiting Jesus. She felt better…not in pain like she did when she was in the intensive care unit. Erin told Molly she wanted to go back to heaven.

Molly left her friend about 3:30 pm that afternoon. That was her last visit. Erin died at 9:00 pm that night. The child sought heaven—a place she found comforting…a place where Jesus would befriend children and where bodily pain and exhaustion would no longer exist.

Research studies of children who go over to the other side and return as Erin did, find that the most common emotion children tell about is feeling happy. They are safe and secure. Children reported feeling comfortable–no longer hurting–even if their illness had caused them pain.

I picked up Joseph and handed the child to his father whose tears washed torrentially down upon his son. I beckoned the father to a chair. The father took a seat rocking his son and snuggling his face down into his son's cheeks and neck. He took in deep breaths like you would when smelling a bouquet of flowers. He inhaled his son's scent. I'd seen this behavior before—those left behind finding comfort in the aroma of the person who died. The chaplain and I shared in these precious moments in silence. Later, I promised the father I would find the clothes the child was wearing at the time of the accident and give them to him. Many parents keep the clothes of their dead children around for a while because the odor imbedded in the material is familiar and comforting. It's okay to do so. This olfactory trace is a soothing memory of the lost child. There are subliminal aroma connections we have with those we've spent time loving and they are intense enough to calm us after the person's death.

A study of mothers illustrates this point. Kids were given new t-shirts and told to run around for a couple hours in them. The shirts were then placed in sealed, unmarked plastic bags. Mothers were lined up and asked to sniff each bag to determine which bag held the t-shirt their child wore. Yes, the mothers could all find the shirts their own children had worn. So keeping the clothing of the deceased around can be a good thing, a comfort measure for those left behind. Aromas can lead us back to some good memories.

"I am glad you told me the story about the little girl," the father said. "It gives me a better picture to hold on to. I am glad the girl said there is no pain. I fiercely want to believe Joseph did not suffer as the truck hit the car. He's just a little boy. If I can picture him with Jesus, and without pain, maybe I can go on."

We went on to see his six-year-old son who was sleeping. The father did not awaken the child although he pulled him into his arms and smothered him with wet kisses. The father was in shock. His sorrow was raw. The rage inside him mixed with an overwhelming agony. He shook his head and rubbed his forehead as if to clear away the horrendous picture playing inside his mind.

I met the mother the day after the car accident. A morphine pump pulsed narcotic medication into her bloodstream. She looked like a marionette with her legs attached to ropes and pulleys secured with weights at the foot of her bed and her re-set arms cradled in casts within conforming foam troughs placed around them.

I explained my background to the mother and the reason for my visit--to answer any questions she had and support her over the next few weeks as best I could. I knew she was told before surgery by the coroner that her four-year old son died instantly. I told her we did not have to talk now. I could come back. I left the time for any conversation up to her. I imagined her thoughts were elsewhere.

But I was wrong. She looked up at me and asked, without hesitation, if I was sure Joseph was dead. As I sat down beside her bed, I said, "Yes, I am sorry." I knew that I would, if in her circumstances, also ask a nurse again if my child were really dead just to be certain. "I sleep with the nightmare and when I wake up, the nightmare begins again," she confided. "My mind keeps slipping back to the crash," she said. She asked me if I thought Joseph suffered in the end. I told her that my understanding of what happens at death came from patients I cared for who were declared clinically dead by doctors but returned to life. These people said that when a motor vehicle accident occurred, they instantaneously floated out of their bodies away from the wreck and went forward toward a great light-being that radiated love. They said they felt no discomfort even though their bodies were smashed and torn apart. I said I imagined Joseph traveled out of his body without pain toward the light-being. I told her that when people die they are met by loved ones on the other side who welcome them into heaven. And this was all I could tell her then. Post anesthesia sedatives and sleepiness blessedly took hold of her and her eyelids closed as I got these last words out. I hoped she knew her son was not in pain, and that he was somewhere good.

The next day I found the father sitting at the mother's bedside. The chaplain was with them. She kneeled down and quoted comforting Psalms to the couple whose hands and fingers clutched each other in a tense grip as they listened.

The Lord is near to the brokenhearted and saves the crushed in spirit.

Psalm 34:18

He heals the brokenhearted and binds up their wounds.

Psalm 147:3

The parents asked the chaplain for guidance as to what to tell their son who lived. She told them that often parents will let a young child know that their sibling will no longer be with them but will be with Jesus in a beautiful place they all will visit someday. The chaplain said this would give the child hope and allow him to envision his brother as happy. The chaplain said Joseph was alive in another place.

The chaplain quoted scriptures saying:

But we do not want you to be uninformed, brothers, about those who are asleep, that you may not grieve as others do who have no hope. For since we believe that Jesus died and rose again, even so, through Jesus, God will bring with him those who have fallen asleep.

1 Thessalonians 4:13

The mother looked at me and said, "But he asks me when his brother is coming back. How can I make a six-year-old understand?" She sought specific instructions about how to talk to her son.

I suggested the mother create a story in which the child could picture his brother the last time he saw him. In the past, I had used the visual image of a balloon to represent the spirit of someone who died. In such a narrative, at the time of the car crash,

Joseph's spiritual form rises out of the car like a balloon soaring upward into the sky.

For children, balloons mark special, happy occasions and their floating away forever is a familiar scene for a six-year-old. The child could step into the story and see what happened unfold.

A few days later, the mother told me she was happy to see Joseph's brother smile as he pictured his brother gliding away when she told him the balloon story. With this story, she had created a space a six-year-old mind could enter and see his brother as happy. For a time, the mother could set aside her pain.

I visited the parents the remaining weeks the mother was hospitalized. I watched them crying into the sleeves of their clothes to muffle the sounds coming from their hearts. Their loss replayed endlessly over and over. The father said, "We are so empty." The couple held hands—their grip a sign of protectiveness for each other. I looked at them and thought, "Everyone wants to feel love like that." I observed them seemingly determined to set aside their inner turmoil as they mourned the loss of one son while loving the child that lived.

I witnessed them animatedly playing with their six-year old son. It had to be scary to love this other child so very much and know life is unfair and he also could be taken away in a flash. The couple somehow found the strength to set aside their grief to love. They were moving forward. I knew nothing could change what happened. Nothing could make it better. But, maybe, just maybe, the stories of children who went over and came back made these parents stronger to face life without Joseph with them here.

Just before I was assigned as a nurse to these parents, I talked extensively with a man who had lost a son when the child was seventeen. He voiced what other parents echo about the loneliness they faced when their child died. In the beginning, friends gathered at the funeral and dropped off food and flowers at the father's home. But as time went on, buddies distanced themselves from what happened. This man and his friends still got together to bowl and play cards. But the friends never mentioned his son.

Time does not take away the pain of losing a child. This man—ten years since the death of his son—is elated when someone remembers his son and says his son's name aloud. His is overjoyed when friends or family tell stories of happy times with his son. A parent never lets go of a child who has died.

People often don't talk with parents about a child who has died because such conversation is awkward. Acquaintances and family members do not want to bring parents to tears. Dodging the topic seems kind. In addition, we know that people may not discuss the death of a child with parents because it brings the possibility of losing a child too close to home. This hesitation to confront what has happened is not an intentional slight. Rather, it seems a subconscious personal preservation mechanism. By disassociating themselves, family and friends construct in their minds a seemingly protective shield that wards off loss of a child happening to them.

So it occurred to me, I would be remiss if I did not share what one parent expressed about the discomfort of dialogue with a family that might also face the same. To better prepare them for the road ahead, at our last visit, I talked with the mother and father about this clumsiness of our society's manners around death of a child. I told them that they might need to let people know it was okay to talk about Joseph with them. Simply saying, "We like hearing your stories about times with our son," could elicit

treasured remembrances. I shared with them this
scripture:

> And God shall wipe away all tears from their
> eyes; and there shall be no more death,
> neither sorrow, nor crying, neither shall there
> be any more pain: for the former things are
> passed away.

> *Revelation 21:4*

Destiny

Show me, O LORD, my life's end and the number of my days; let me know how fleeting is my life. You have made my days a mere handbreadth; the span of my years is as nothing before you. Each man's life is but a breath. Selah. Man is a mere phantom as he goes to and fro: He bustles about, but only in vain; he heaps up wealth, not knowing who will get it. But now, Lord, what do I look for? My hope is in you.

Psalm 39:4-7

It was a muggy, hot July evening. Michael, a burly 59-year-old man had driven 500 miles home feeling nauseous and lightheaded but not realizing he had suffered a second heart attack. Arriving at the emergency room (ER) all sweaty with an ache in his chest, he balked when the physician said, "I am placing you in a coronary care unit (intensive care unit) until we can determine for sure the extent of damage your heart has suffered."

Michael's disbelief came from the fact he had open heart surgery and three vessels sewn onto his heart the previous November. That year, after a big Thanksgiving feast with family, he experienced crushing chest pain. Michael winced and clutched his chest when he tried to stand up from dinner. He was unable to hide his discomfort with his usual life-of-the-party humor. He needed the help of family members to walk to the car. That evening at the ER, Michael acquiesced to tests and gave the okay for surgery. There was nothing else he could do.

Now, Michael took a deep breath and told the medical staff, "My stomach kind of hurt…felt knotted up. I bent over and held onto the bar. It seemed to me I might have the beginnings of an ulcer. I did a lot of drinking entertaining clients at the convention in Indianapolis." With an anger laced but measured voice Michael pointed at the doctor and ranted, "I did not think I could have another heart attack. I thought the open-heart surgery and bypass grafts took care of that possibility. I recall I paid a good bit for your services which now do not seem to have worked."

The doctor did not response in kind to Michael's heated statement. He just accepted the words for what they were—a man's denial that surgery could only do so much and the needed lifestyle changes must come from within the patient. The doctor understood that Michael had just realized he might be a step closer to death than he had ever been before. A "little death" of the heart muscle, as occurs with a heart attack, brings mortality up close and personal. Heart attacks scare people.

The doctor called me to consult with Michael. As I walked into the room, Michael, rebuffed his own part in the unfolding critical situation now playing out within him, and declared loudly, "God knows how I ended up in this place again." I was hearing the words of a person going through the stages of loss and grief...his anger...his denial. Could I talk this patient through another "little death" to acceptance where he would better be able to recover? All I knew is that I had to try.

Destinies are partly determined by chance and luck. Michael could not expunge the genes he inherited that predisposed him to heart disease. That was chance. His occupation was regional sales manager for a heavy equipment company. People would say this was luck. Michael was one of the fortunate ones to earn in the six digits traveling over a five-state region for a company that treated its employees to cruises as bonuses for sales. Men and women would say he had a dream job. And so Michael had thought.

I explained the purpose of my visit— to give him someone with whom to talk. Michael laughed, "You mean someone to tell my troubles to?" "Tell me about the real you," I joked light-heartedly.

"I'm a family man with a lovely second wife and blended family of five. I love them all and I provide a decent life for them. Two kids completed college. Two are in college. The surprise child is in high school. They've had every opportunity. I made sure they did because I grew up always on the edge watching others take part in activities my parents could not afford for us. My kids all play musical instruments and are active in sports. I grew up on the sidelines watching other kids. My wife has a weekly tennis lesson and is involved in neighborhood projects."

"Sounds like a busy family," I commented. "What do you do besides work?" I asked. "Me?" said Michael. "I told you. I am the breadwinner. I work 12-hour days, six days a week. I bask in their happiness."

"Tell me," I said, "What would happen if you slowed your work down?" Michael replied, "I can't. Too much rests on me. I wouldn't know any good way to keep up the way we live besides my work. In fact, if you excuse me, I need to make some calls."

Michael's condition required surgery. I stopped in after he was transferred out of the intensive care unit. I opened the conversation with a question that allowed Michael to say anything. "How's it going?" He surprised me with his answer. "This is going to sound crazy, but you asked. I can tell you because your job is to listen, right?" "Right," I concurred.

Michael went on to recount his experience during open-heart surgery a day ago. "I was wheeled into the operating room and I remember the doctor saying, 'In just a minute, you will be asleep.' The next thing I knew I was looking down on my body from a place up high above the operating table. There was music playing and lots of chatter among the doctors and nurses. Then things got hazy all around and I found myself drifting higher and away from the scene toward a bright light. I wasn't scared. A booming voice bellowed, 'What have you done with your life to show me?' I could only see the light so I was unsure who was talking to me. I hesitated. The voice spoke again saying, 'You will live. You are in heaven but I want you to return and teach your children about Me.' The next thing I knew a nurse was telling me to roll over. My surgery had ended. I was in the intensive care unit. So, you were the one who asked how it is going. Tell me I'm not nuts. Is this something you've heard before?"

I explained that some patients who have clinically died and come back, such as those experiencing cardiopulmonary resuscitation (CPR), tell nurses God has spoken to them and given them a task to do. Of course, the only patients we hear from are the ones that are told to return. The assignments vary. One person told me he was to take care of his elderly parents.

Another woman was told to forgive her ex-husband. "My read on your experience," I said, "is that you have been asked to add some religion to the many things you've given your children. You are not the first person to be asked to do this."

Michael frowned and stated, "Since I woke up from surgery, thoughts of God have been banging on my head trying to get in. I feel like such a hypocrite. In my 20s, I moved away from God. I set aside the faith my parents instilled in me and I concentrated on providing my children with the tangible things …the sports camps, the cars, the parties. Growing up, I went to school with well-to-do kids. Looking in from outside their circle, I thought that people with money had no problems. I wanted my kids to have that kind of life. Only now do I recognize I had a warped picture of what was important to give my family. My mother used to say, 'Old so soon. Smart so late.' Can't imagine why God would want anything to do with me. Am I too late? Do you think I can ever find God again?"

"You shouldn't wonder," I said. "Everyone is important to God. You can forget God. God does not forget you. God will find you. Destinies are partly determined by chance and luck but also by wisdom and grace. God's door is always open."

I shared Matthew 18:12-14:

If a man owns a hundred sheep, and one of them wanders away, will he not leave the ninety-nine on the hills and go look for the one that wandered off? And if he finds it, I tell you the truth, he is happier about that one sheep than about the ninety-nine that did not wander off. In the same way, your Father in Heaven is not willing that any of these little ones should be lost.

Matthew 18:12-14

Then we prayed *The Prayer of St. Francis* which says:

Lord, make me an instrument of your peace. Where there is hatred, let me sow love; Where there is injury, pardon; Where there is discord, harmony; Where there is error, truth; Where there is doubt, faith; Where there is despair, hope; Where there is darkness, light; And where there is sadness, joy. O Divine Master, Grant that I may not so much seek to be consoled as to console; To be understood as to understand; To be loved as to love. For it is in giving, we receive; it is in pardoning that we are pardoned; and it is in dying that we are born to eternal life.

I gave him a copy of the prayer and said I would come back the next day.

When I stopped back in to see Michael, he was ready to talk. "Shut the door, please. I've been reading the prayer you left with me. I want to do what God asked. No one is guaranteed a tomorrow. Will you help me now?"

I knew what Michael was asking. Here in the shadow of death he narrowly escaped, he wanted a route out. I had been with many patients before who decided after experiencing a sacred event, as Michael had, that they needed help turning their life around. That was my job. I said I could help.

Michael told me, "I thought I would get it all in life. But now I see I was peddling on a conveyor belt of more and more possessions. Belongings I once considered luxuries became necessities. The image I had of myself was a successful businessman. I thought I was too smart, too busy for religion. Now I ask you…who am I?"

I responded, "You are a man seeking to be a good presence in this world. What you have done you did in the spirit of being a good father and a good provider. Now you see that more is expected. But, with a plan, you can do it. *The Prayer of St. Francis* is comforting because it reminds us that when we are wrong, we can change. It tells us we will be led out of the darkness into light. Life is a process of seeking to understand ourselves. The circumstances of our lives teach us. The people we meet help us learn better who we are. God told you during your open-heart surgery to tell your children about the love of God. We take no material possessions with us when we die. Love is what endures into the next life. The life we have on earth is like a classroom in which we learn. These are lessons you can teach your children."

"So I'm not such a bad guy?" Michael quipped. "No, you are just like the rest of us human beings," I replied. With these principles established, Michael and I dialogued about some conversations he wanted to have first with his wife and then with his children. We role-played what he would say. He took some notes and said he would reflect on them. Writing thoughts down sometimes helps a person find just the right words when the time comes to have an emotion-laden talk. I gave Michael the card of a chaplain who did home visits and could be with him during discussions if he wished.

This man, who at first denied his illness, coped well with the new directive he was given during open heart surgery. When discharged from the hospital, he left a note for me. It said, "Thank you for listening and accepting my story as true. Thank you for believing in me and letting me know I am just human and God is a loving, forgiving being. I shall tell all. I will teach my children. I have been conforming to society. Now I will work on developing a spiritual life to prepare me for heaven."

I was reminded how God speaks to those who listen, and this Bible verse came to mind:

The unfolding of your words gives light.

Psalm 119:13

Peace Be With You

For we know that if the earthly tent we live in is destroyed, we have a building from God, an eternal house in heaven, not built by human hands. Meanwhile we groan, longing to be clothed instead with our heavenly dwelling, because when we are clothed, we will not be found naked. For while we are in this tent, we groan and are burdened, because we do not wish to be unclothed but to be clothed instead with our heavenly dwelling, so that what is mortal may be swallowed up by life. Now the one who has fashioned us for this very purpose is God, who has given us the Spirit as a deposit, guaranteeing what is to come.

2 Corinthians:1-5

The nurse who called me said she was concerned that a patient was refusing essential medication, and without it, she would die. She said the patient's daughter could use some support dealing with her mother's reluctance to go on living. I discovered the nurse would benefit from some assistance too.

When the nurses brought her medications the first day of hospitalization, Elizabeth refused them. The doctor told nurses to hold off and give the woman time to adjust. After reviewing the importance of the medications with the patient this morning and again being turned down, the nurse felt a clinical nurse specialist might be able to sort out the situation.

When I got to the cardiac unit, the nurse told me she was confused about the situation. Earlier in the day, the nurse lingered in the patient's ante room putting away some medications. She overheard Elizabeth, an 80-year-old mother pleading with her daughter to not interfere in her dying. The nurse listened as the mother made clear she had made a decision that she felt was her choice to make.

"Let me go," the mother pleaded. "I am tired and I am ready. I need you to help me with this because I know you can make them stop me. Jesus is waiting for me. Always remember that story I told you about me dying before. I have been to heaven and back. I am not afraid. You have come whenever I needed you to help me get medical treatments. I need you to not rescue me this one last time. I know this is hard. I am asking this of you knowing you are strong."

The daughter was quiet for several minutes but then said that she would abide by her mother's wishes. The nurse witnessed the mother and daughter embrace and both say simultaneously, "I love you so very much." The daughter did not lift a hand to wipe her tears and drops cascaded onto both of them when they hugged.

The nurse said, "There was peace in the room. It was the most beautiful moment I've felt between a mother and a daughter. There was a space encircling them no one else could enter. The daughter did not want her mother to die. But the daughter respected her mother's wishes enough to release her to go her own way." The nurse stepped out of the ante room into the hallway knowing the mother and daughter would not want to know this personal exchange had been witnessed.

The nurse indicated that I could find the mother resting in her room. The daughter had gone to the chapel. The patient had arrived by ambulance the day before after fainting at home. Neither the ambulance crew nor her husband followed her request that she be allowed to stay home.

I found Elizabeth lying in bed. She was a tiny woman weighing only 78 pounds. Her slight figure was dwarfed by the hospital bed. Only her repeated movements interlacing her fingers into a prayer-like steeple told me she was awake. I introduced myself. Elizabeth opened her eyes, saw me, and shut them. To ease any awkwardness, I asked her permission to sit down. She politely replied, "Sure." I explained that the nurses wanted me to explore with her why she was declining medications including one necessary to prevent a pulmonary embolism. The woman's heart was beating in a pattern called atrial fibrillation. She needed a daily dose of a medication targeted to prevent clotting. Without the medication, she was more likely to experience a clot in her heart breaking off and floating to her lungs. Such a condition is life-threatening.

Elizabeth said she was sorry for all the trouble. She asked me to apologize to the nurses noting she realized they were just doing their jobs. "I suspect the nurse on today heard us talking and called you," she whispered. "Yes," I replied. "The nurse was concerned about what she overheard in your mother-daughter conversation this morning."

The woman pleaded, "Please don't make it any harder on my daughter than it already is. I ask that of you. I am so weak. My son had to carry me up the stairs to my bedroom after I had my weekly blood draw. I cannot bear that. I cannot be a burden. I know I could die of a pulmonary embolism. I have awoken at night with the room spinning. I have thought that maybe my heart was shooting out a clot or two then. It does not frighten me."

Elizabeth began unwinding spindles of memories blending all the ages she'd ever been. I did not interrupt as this story of her life unfolded before me. "Times were tough during the war but my family persevered. We sold rags and newspapers. Mom worked at a thrift shop in exchange for clothes. I learned to clean houses when I was twelve. I was sent here and there. I did what I was told. During the war, I got a job in a factory. I knew my working was helping feed our family of ten. I got married when I found someone who was responsible and a hard worker. We built a good life. We moved out of the city and bought our first house when we had two children. I felt like I had it all. I was working Mondays through Fridays. On Saturdays, I did the wash, cleaned and got the groceries. Marriage was like that back then. It's what a woman did. However, on Sundays, I sometimes didn't go to church. It was my real day of rest."

"The kids grew up. They weren't particularly close. Even after all that time together when they were young, they each had their own personality. I guess that is to be expected. As adults, they all came home for holidays and were polite to each other, dad and me. I am thankful for that. Wish they could have been better friends. Love doesn't always go the way you hope. Love can be both beautiful and heartbreaking. A family picture doesn't tell you that, does it? But, I'm okay. Everyone gets a different bag of genes and has to carry on with the traits of parents and other ancestors. How funny I expected my children to be more like me. They are in many ways and, in others, not. The exception is my daughter. She has become like me. And that is why I can trust her to understand my thoughts and beliefs."

"When my daughter was in college, I was not feeling so good. I was working hard, drinking and smoking. One evening my stomach hurt to beat the band. I collapsed. My husband phoned my daughter who told him to hang up and dial, "911". I remember them lifting me onto the cart and, then, nothing else until I awoke in the operating room. I was looking down from a space above the surgical table. There I lay. The doctors were talking. I heard one say, 'She's not going to make it.'"

"I didn't seem to care what that doctor said. I was floating up away from the doctors and nurses. I found myself drawn toward a very bright light. Not just drawn but pulled. The light came all around me and seemed to carry me down a tunnel. I was not afraid. At the end of the tunnel, my aunt who died 20 years before, appeared. I used to clean her house when she was too old to do so herself. 'Dear,' she said, 'you are in heaven, but you need to go back." A voice I believe was Jesus, declared, 'Your family needs you still. It is not your time. I will make a place for you when it is your time.'"

"The surgeon who came to see me the next day said my heart stopped during the operation. He thought they had lost me. I didn't tell him I could hear and see what was going on in surgery. I didn't tell him about Jesus. That is something you just don't share with many people. But, I did tell my daughter.

After an experience like this, a person sees differently. Now I am sure about heaven. I know God is for real. I am tired. My pains are blurring my happy memories. I want to feel the love I felt surround me when my heart stopped during surgery. It is there I want to go. I want that happiness. I am looking forward to the journey ahead."

What does a nurse say when a dying person explains how life and death works? Death is both a physical and a spiritual experience. I extended my hand. Elizabeth took it and rubbed it a little and put it down. I said, "Thank you." I offered to pray with her and folded my hands in hers saying:

Dear God, we ask that you bring comfort to Elizabeth who is ill and tired. She loves you and wishes to journey beyond this life. May the words of *Matthew 11:28* which say, *Come to me, all you who are weary and burdened, and I will give you rest,* comfort her. Please stay by her side. In Jesus' name. Amen.

I found the daughter in the chapel. No one else was there. We talked. Through tear-filled eyes, she explained, "Life has been hard for her. The war. The poverty. The deaths of her brothers and sisters. The sickness and death of her first daughter. There's a saying, 'Falling down is part of life. Getting back up is living.' She did that for a long time but she does not want to do it anymore. She was always cheerful, never complaining. She has been giving away things to me over the past six months while she has been on hospice. It seems she has wanted to become lighter, unencumbered by possessions but looking forward to the presence of them in my life. Now I see she was getting herself ready to go. I am grateful she has been able to handle leaving on her own terms. That is important for her. I've been blessed by this time to say good-bye.

Did she tell you she was in heaven once? Her journey has been hard. Death is her light. She is at peace now. Perhaps, for the very first time, in a long while, she can rest."

Back at the nurses' station, I smiled at the nurse who called me. "Yes, that had to be one of the most beautiful moments a nurse could see between a mother and daughter. Thanks for letting me know.

There were some unsettled issues. They have untangled them. They reached an understanding that in life you have to be able to distinguish what to accept and what to not bear. If you are okay, I am going to leave things be. Their two hearts are one." The nurse nodded in agreement saying, 'I admire the mother's convictions and the daughter's love.'"

Nurses respect patient choices even when different from their own. While needing to educate the patient about the consequences of not taking her medication, the nurse in this story focused on respecting Elizabeth's wishes.

What a gift it is to be able to say one last time to someone dying, "I love you."

Q & A with the Author

1. You have written books about near-death experiences. Why now do you write a Bible-based book?

Now that I am no longer constrained by employment in public entities, I am free to reveal the relationship patients have told me exists between earthly life and heaven. I believe Bible passages guide and comfort patients and their loved ones.

2. The Journal of Christian Nursing recently published an article written by you. In it, you encourage nurses to integrate use of scriptures at the bedside. What is the key message of this manuscript?

Nurses are ideally suited to partner with clergy in reading from the Bible. Many anxieties and fears can be relieved when patients hear scriptures.

3. You talk about heaven as a place where people meet and talk to God. I must assume that you believe in God and Jesus. Do you?

Yes, heaven is the afterlife where people make contact with a being of unconditional love often reported as God or Jesus. Survivors of death say God gives them instructions such as "Go back and teach your children about God and Jesus." I have known God and Jesus for as long as I can remember. Jesus was a great teacher. He used stories to teach people.

As an educator I believe in teaching through storytelling. Students need not only information but also the understanding of how the facts apply to real people situations. Stories of patients provide a background on which to tack knowledge.

4. You studied what values people want to be remembered for once they make it onward to heaven. You stated that most people want their sons and daughters, their family and loved ones to know the principles and ideals upon which they based their lives. How might you suggest that people let their loved ones know?

First, by living those values. People are not just who they say they are, or who others say they are. How people interact with others shows who they really are.

Kindness is a value we can see borne out in a person's actions. Generosity can be observed. Truth can be understood.

Second, by discussing their values with their family and friends. People can start by talking about why they have lived the way they chose to live. A person might start the conversation by saying, "I did this because I value (honesty, friendship)."

"I always follow these precepts because I want to be (law-abiding, true to my church)."

"I did this because I was scared inside and wanted to feel secure."

Discussions of values teach others how to look at situations and decide what action to take based on who they are and who they want to be. We, of course, do not always live up to our own expectations. And, sometimes, only hindsight tells us why we did something the way we chose to do it.

5. This book reveals scripture passages about light from the Bible. How did you come to know these?

I became an oblate (community member) of the Benedictine Holy Wisdom Monastery in Madison, Wisconsin. Days there were spent in work, study, reflection and prayer. As a nurse, I heard many patients talk about the light. I opened a Bible resource manual at the monastery and wrote down passages about light out of curiosity to better understand if the stories people who reported near-death experiences told me about the light were the same as what the Bible would suggest.

6. Are you confident that heaven exists?

I know heaven exists. Getting there does not require unblemished conduct or works of greatness. We just need openness to the Lord God who is seeking us.

About the Author

Susan L. Schoenbeck RN, MSN holds a master's degree in Nursing from the University of Wisconsin- Madison.

Schoenbeck has received the Universal Voice Award along with many excellences in teaching awards and writing honors. Her manuscripts have been published in many peer-reviewed journals. She is a member of the International Association for Near-Death Studies (IANDS). Her research on near-death experiences is reported in the IANDS journal.

Schoenbeck volunteers as PR Chair for the American Legion Auxiliary Post 66 and at the Sahuarita Food Bank. She mentors nursing students with English as a second language for Walla Walla University.

Schoenbeck is author of:

The Final Entrance: Journeys beyond Life

Near-Death Experiences: Visits to the Other Side

Good Grief: Daily Meditations: A Book of Caring and Remembrance

Zen and the Art of Nursing

Learn more about Susan Schoenbeck at susanschoenbeck.com. Watch Susan's website for links to Instagram and blog.

32258926R00102

Made in the USA
San Bernardino, CA
12 April 2019